D1
and
CHILDREN

Answers to the Questions that Parents
and Children Ask to Help Survive
Divorce and Find Happiness

Brian Harris, B.A., M.Ed.

Copyright © 2016 by Brian Harris

All rights reserved. This book, or parts thereof,
may not be reproduced in any form
without written permission from the publisher.

ISBN # 978-1530001613

Every effort has been made to ensure that the information
contained in this book is accurate. Neither the publisher
nor the author is engaged in rendering professional advice
or services to the individual reader. The ideas, strategies
and suggestions contained in this book are not intended
as a substitute for consulting with appropriate professionals.
Neither the author nor the publisher shall be liable or
responsible for any loss or damage allegedly arising
from any information or suggestions in this book.

CGS Communications, Inc.

CONTENTS

	Introduction	5
1.	The Problem	13
2.	Questions that Parents Ask	21
3.	Questions that Kids Ask	119
4.	Some Final Thoughts	169

"There is no such thing as a 'broken family'. Family is family, and is not determined by marriage certificates, divorce papers, and adoption documents. Families are made in the heart. The only time family becomes null is when those ties in the heart are cut. If you cut those ties, those people are not your family. If you make those ties, those people are your family. And if you hate those ties, those people will still be your family because whatever you hate will always be with you."
C. JoyBell C.

INTRODUCTION

Rosemary was a grade 1 student when her parents separated. This was not a happy separation (is there really such a thing?). Her father left unexpectedly. Her mother entered a world of self-absorption, wildly swinging between anger and denial. Rosemary came to school day after day in tears. She would often sit in class, staring at the walls, most of the time refusing to participate in any activities. *(Note: Whenever I use names throughout the book, the names are fictitious although the case studies are a compilation of actual case studies I have been involved with).*

Quickly Rosemary began to fall behind in her schoolwork which contributed to her feelings of unhappiness. One month after the initial separation, Rosemary no longer wanted to come to school. She woke up with severe stomach aches and begged her mother to stay home from work to take care of her. Her mother, having already used a number of sick days due to her own anguish, further jeopardized her own job by staying home with her daughter. Two months after the separation, Rosemary had missed almost one month of school. Her mother was one step away from losing her job. Their world was spiraling out of control.

Fast forward twenty-five years later and Rosemary is now a very successful professional, happily married with children of her own. Her mother has been remarried for the past fifteen years, a relationship that brings her joy and stability. You might ask "How did Rosemary make such a significant change in her life?" The strategies that were used to help Rosemary are outlined in this book. They can help you to assist your children in surviving divorce and becoming happy and successful.

> *"Someone was hurt before you, wronged before you, hungry before you, frightened before you.. yet, someone survived.. You can do anything you choose to do."*
> Maya Angelou

Mark's parents separated when he was thirteen. After the initial anger and grief, it was decided that Mark would spend equal time living with each parent. This seemed like a good arrangement that considered the need for both parents to still be involved in the life of their son. Unfortunately, both parents quickly jumped back into the dating scene leaving Mark often alone at home.

Within six months of the divorce, Mark stopped doing any homework. He started drinking which soon led to the use of drugs. Less than a year after the initial separation, Mark was not only failing at school; he had a growing dependence on drugs. During this year, he also began to associate with older teenagers who had dropped out of school.

By fifteen, Mark was breaking into houses to support his drug habit. By nineteen, Mark vanished. He became a drifter who still some ten years later had no contact with his parents. What happened to Mark? Did his parents do something wrong? How can you help to prevent your children from growing up like Mark? Answers to these questions will be explored in this book.

Divorce affects almost one out of every two families in America. Rarely are divorces amicable in the way that some celebrity couples would like us to believe. Divorce is a form of loss. Many experts suggest that divorce is a little less painful than having your best friend die. There are even some who would say that the pain caused by divorce is worse than losing a friend because death is final whereas divorce can continue to raise any unresolved issues for the rest of your life.

This book will show you how to identify the stages that you and your children can expect to experience as you deal with divorce. Such an understanding can be very helpful to you as you attempt to guide your children through the emotional trauma of divorce. Understanding how people grieve can help you and your children to emerge from a divorce as stronger and happier people.

Research studies from a few decades ago often concluded that children were often crippled by divorce. The research stated that the children of divorce exhibited greater mental health issues as well as greater problems in forming positive adult relationships. In this book I will not only talk about this research, but I will talk about the current research findings as they relate to the children of divorce. I will look at how both you and your children can find happiness after divorce.

While there are no perfect answers that are guaranteed to help every child who experiences separation and divorce, I will share strategies and tips in this book that I have seen make a positive difference in the lives of others (and while I use the word divorce primarily in this book, my comments also apply to what happens during the "separation" before a divorce).

"Courage doesn't always roar. Sometimes courage is the little voice at the end of the day that says I'll try again tomorrow."
Mary Anne Radmacher

As a school counselor for more than twenty years, I often wondered why some children of divorce found happiness and success while others lived a life of pain and failure. How was it that some kids who experienced divorce struggled to get out of bed in the morning while others were happy, well-adjusted students who had a strong group of friends and a bright future? We will explore the answers to these question throughout this book.

In attempting to help the children of divorce, I have conducted support groups within several schools. I have also presented workshops for both parents and teachers (and counselors) related to helping children better deal with divorce. The questions we will be looking at in this book are those that both children and adults most frequently asked me in the workshops that I presented.

While many of the experts are sometimes in conflict regarding the impact of divorce on children, my experience tells me that the majority of kids initially suffer some form of pain, anger, denial, anxiety, and confusion. This can result in unhappiness, depression, and can most certainly affect grades at school as well as causing a strain in their relationship with others.

It is my experience that most kids will survive divorce and become happy successful adults. On the other hand, some kids will get trapped in the anguish and hopelessness of divorce causing them to experience unhappiness and a lack of success in much that they do.

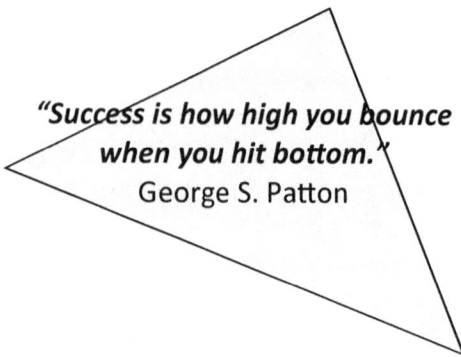

"Success is how high you bounce when you hit bottom."
George S. Patton

While no one can guarantee a 100% success rate in helping the children of divorce, there are some basic strategies and approaches that have worked successfully for others. Often the best way to achieve success is to observe what other successful people have done and then copy them.

It is my intent that this book will help to outline these strategies and approaches that others have successfully used with their children. It is my hope that these strategies and approaches can provide a foundation for you to help your children. Whenever I conduct workshops for parents or students, it is often the questions that are asked that result in the greatest learning. As a result of this, I have written this book in a question and answer format

As you consider the thoughts provided within this

book, I can't emphasize enough the importance of consulting with a trained professional to assist you in helping your children to better deal with a divorce. Every child is unique. While there can be some similarities as to what happens during a divorce, different children can react in different ways. Sometimes as parents we get so caught up in our grief that it's difficult for us to help our children. Sometimes as parents we feel so guilty about the pain we have caused our kids that we fail to do what is best for them. In such situations a professional counsellor might be able to help you and your children deal with the divorce in a more positive manner.

A frequent complaint I often hear from children and teenagers is that they worry about their parents when a divorce occurs, that they often find themselves becoming a "parent" to their parents. I believe the content of this book can help you to be a better parent, to be the kind of parent that your children will respect, and the kind of parent who will make a positive difference in the lives of your children.

"The only thing more unthinkable than leaving was staying; the only thing more impossible than staying was leaving. I didn't want to destroy anything or anybody. I just wanted to slip quietly out the back door, without causing any fuss or consequences, and then not stop running until I reached Greenland."
Elizabeth Gilbert, *"Eat, Pray, Love"*

The Problem

1. What is the current rate of divorce in North America?

The rate of divorce in North America (Canada and the U.S.) is often quoted to be somewhere a little under 50%. In other words, almost one out of every two marriages will end in divorce. In reality this number might actually be higher if we take into account "separations" (which can still impact both adults and children in a negative manner) where some separations end in a reconciliation preventing a divorce.

In addition, in considering the statistics related to divorce, the number of marriages is decreasing (more people are living together without getting married) which means that when "unmarried" couples separate, these numbers will not show up in divorce statistics. Recently a woman told me that her live-in partner of twelve years had left her. They had three children together. These kids will suffer the pain of a "divorce" and their two parents will likely go through a legal process of dividing assets and determining living arrangements for the children as though they were going through a divorce, yet a separation like this will not show up in any divorce statistics.

Similarly, a fifteen year-old boy told me that his parents divorced when he was two. Since that time his mother had six different men live with her (and her son). Each time that these men left, to be replaced by someone new, the boy was over and over again experiencing the effects of a divorce even though these separations would never show up in any statistics on divorce because the mother had never actually remarried.

More children are affected by divorce than the official statistics on divorce show. While divorce is the legal dissolution of a marriage, there are a wide variety of family situations where a divorce never occurred because the two parents were never married, yet the children still suffer from what happened.

In researching several sources for this book, I found that divorce in the USA for a first marriage is in the range of 41 - 50% depending on the study. For second marriages, the divorce rate is 60 - 67%; and for third marriages the divorce rate is 74 - 74%. In Canada, a 2012 article in the Globe and Mail stated that the current rate of divorce in Canada is approximately 38 - 41%.

Whichever statistics you accept related to divorce, the reality is that divorce directly affects almost half the population in North America, and indirectly impacts almost everyone because it is difficult not be exposed to the results of someone else's divorce. Some kids in non-divorced families experience "divorce like" symptoms when their parents argue. The children of continually married parents may encounter unusual anxiety when their parents have disagreements because of the perceived threat of a divorce even though the reality might never happen.

2. Does divorce always cause problems for children?

In looking at several studies related to the impact of divorce on children, I found the following:

- 12% of children of married parents visit a psychologist; 25% of the children of divorce visit a psychologist

- children of divorce have a two times higher risk to run into "problems"

- children of divorce tend to experience lower success in their performance at school

In my experience with children, I believe that divorce has an impact on all children initially, and for most kids that impact is negative. Fortunately, given the resiliency of children, better parenting, a lessening adversarial approach to the legalities of divorce, and better support systems for the children of divorce, I believe that most children can recover in a positive manner.

In a 2013 article titled "Is Divorce Bad For Children" in *Scientific American*, the author stated, "Researchers have found that only a relatively small percentage of children experience serious problems in the wake of divorce or later as adults."

While statistically, approximately one out of every two students in the schools where I have worked had experienced divorce, there were nowhere near this many students experiencing problems that could be attributed to a divorce. In some situations, where a student's lack of school success or lack of appropriate behavior was attributed to a "messy" divorce, the reality was that the students already had school related concerns before the divorce occurred. For children who are already experiencing difficulties at school, a divorce can increase these problems.

A mother recently told me how her eleven year-old daughter was struggling with her schoolwork. The mother blamed her daughter's problems at school on a recent divorce, although she went on to explain that her daughter hated to read. In fact, the mother also hated to read. There were few books in their house. The more we talked, the more apparent it became that the child was not struggling at school because of a divorce; rather, she was struggling because she lacked the appropriate reading skills to be successful.

What then are the consequences for children of divorced parents? Will all these children develop school problems? Will all these children develop self-esteem concerns? Will all these children exhibit behavioral problems? Will all these children grow up experiencing increased problems in their relationships with others as adults? Both the research and my extensive experiences as a teacher and a counselor would answer "NO" to these questions.

In the book *For Better or For Worse: Divorce Reconsidered,* the authors Mavis Hetherington and John Kelly, describe a 25 year study related to children of divorce. Their findings stated that only 15% of adult children of divorce experienced problems over and above those from families that did not experience divorce.

3. What are some of the main factors that contribute to children of divorce growing up to be happy and successful adults?

In my experience with thousands of kids who have experienced divorce, there are many factors that affect how children respond to the divorce. These factors can include:

- what was said to them at the time of the divorce?

- were they allowed to express their grief during their loss?

- what are the parenting skills of each parent?

- do they have the appropriate skills and attitude to be successful at school?

- do they have input into their living (custodial) arrangements?

- do they feel loved and accepted?

- are their parents able to let go of their anger and bitterness towards their ex-spouse?

- do their parents set a positive example for dealing with the divorce in appropriate, healthy ways?

- do they have someone to talk to who is impartial and can help them deal with their emotions?

Based on my experience as a professional counselor and educator, and based on various research studies , I would conclude that most children have a negative reaction initially to divorce (as do their parents), but most children with the appropriate help can survive and become happy and successful.

> *"Even when divorce does not result in long-term damage, it is usually brutally painful. To the boys and girls in my research, divorce seemed cataclysmic and inexplicable. How could a child feel safe in a world where adults had suddenly become untrustworthy?"*
> Mavis Hetherington and John Kelly in
> *"For Better or for Worse: Divorce Reconsidered"*

*"In times of grief and sorrow I will hold you
and rock you and take your grief
and make it my own.
When you cry I cry and when
you hurt I hurt. And together
we will try to hold back the floods
of tears and despair
and make it through
the potholed street of life.*
Nicholas Sparks

Questions that Parents Ask

Whenever I talk to kids who have just experienced divorce, most of them feel as if their world has been destroyed. One thirteen year-old girl said that she felt like "her parents had ripped her in two". A nine year-old told me, "I can't stop crying. What did I do wrong?" And a five year-old boy showed me a picture of himself enclosed in a giant teardrop.

In this chapter, we will look at some of the questions I am often asked by parents to help children overcome some of their painful reactions to divorce. It is my hope that the answers to these questions will help you and your children to find happiness after divorce.

"When a child asks you something, answer him, for goodness sake. But don't make a production of it. Children are children, but they can spot an evasion faster than adults, and evasions simply muddles 'em."
Harper Lee, *"To Kill A Mocking Bird"*

1. What are the stages of grieving and what do they have to do with divorce?

Elisabeth Kubler-Ross was a psychiatrist who was a pioneer in studying how death affected people. She formulated five stages of grief that people may experience after the death of a loved one. Many experts now believe that the five stages of grief that she proposed also relate to other forms of loss such as divorce. In other words, both you and your children may experience some or even all of the following stages of grief as a result of a divorce.

The stages are as follows:

i) denial (disbelief)

ii) anger (shock, numbness)

iii) bargaining (yearning)

iv) depression

v) acceptance (forgiveness)

The stages of grieving will be discussed further in the following questions.

2. Is it normal for children to experience the stages of grieving as a result of a divorce?

Yes, it is not only normal for your children to experience the stages of grieving, but the process can be helpful and healthy for them. Although each family member may experience the intensity and duration of each stage differently, it is none-the-less important for everyone to experience some or all of these stages. Most experts believe that those (both adults and children) who struggle for a long period of time with a divorce are often those who "got stuck" in one of the grieving stages and failed to move on to the next stage.

"People in grief need someone to walk with them without judging them."
Gail Sheehy

In considering the five stages of grieving, it is important to realize that each family member will experience the stages according to his or her own timeframe and needs. It is not necessary to experience all five steps. As each person grieves differently, some members of your family might experience the stages in a different order and intensity than other family members. Some people wear their emotions on their sleeves while others tend to keep things to themselves. With children, it can be very helpful to have a trained counsellor help them understand what they are experiencing.

Experts in the field of grieving often state the importance of letting a child grieve. To help our kids survive divorce and to grow up happy and successful, it is critical that we allow them to mourn their losses. Giving your children permission to experience each of the steps in a grieving process while being there to accept and love them unconditionally might be the greatest thing you can do to help them survive a divorce.

While there is sometimes a tendency to spoil our kids with tangible gifts after a divorce, what they really need is understanding. Although there may times you would like your children to better understand what you are going through, in the end your children will be healthier when your focus is on putting yourself in their shoes.

"I believe the process of going from confusion to understanding is a precious, even emotional, experience that can be the foundation of self-confidence."
Brian Greene

3. How should I tell my children about what is happening?

Most books on divorce state that both parents should sit down with their children to inform them that they are going to separate. Let's be realistic here. How many parents have the composure (at the moment of separating) and impartial communication skills (at the moment of separating) to be able to sit down with their children and calmly talk about what is happening? My guess is that in most cases if two parents had such strong communication skills with each other they would unlikely be separating in the first place.

In many situations, especially with older children, kids will often have an awareness that something is wrong in the marriage. This will be especially true if one person has already moved unexpectedly out of the house or there is constant fighting or endless awkward silence. It is quite possible that your kids might start asking questions before you are ready to talk to them about what is happening. Denying what is happening can destroy the trust of your children. You are better to be as honest as possible even if you don't know exactly what is going to happen next. It is better that your children hear about your "separation" from you, rather than a neighbor or relative.

If you and your spouse are able to sit down with your children and do this together, this could be a positive step to helping your kids see that although you are separating from each other, you are still committed to working together to be the best parents you can be. This can be a healthy first step in helping your kids to adjust to the separation. Having said this, you shouldn't expect that your child's reaction is going to be as calm and as rationale as your announcement to him or her, nor should you expect that each of your children are going to react in the same manner. Keep in mind that you might have known for months, or even years, that you and your spouse were having problems; your kids might have been oblivious to your difficulties. In looking at the stages of grieving, the initial response of most children will be either anger or denial (which can include silence and isolation).

"Denial is the lid on our emotional pressure cooker: the longer we leave it on, the more pressure we build up. Sooner or later, that pressure is bound to pop the lid, and we have an emotional crisis."
Susan Forward

If you and your spouse are unable to tell your children together, then you might have to do this alone. However you tell your children, attempt to choose a time that is private for you and your children. In addition, choose a time when your kids might be most receptive to listening and when they have time to absorb what you are telling them (certainly not fifteen minutes before they are about to go to school). Select a time when no one is rushing to be somewhere else and when there is also time for your children to think about what you have said and are able to respond back to you.

4. What should I tell my children?

It is quite possible that before you sit down with your children to talk to them about your separation that you have already entered one of the steps of grieving yourself. This can make it very difficult for you to rationally explain what is happening. In a situation like this it might be useful to involve a friend or relative who your child feels comfortable being with. This person might better explain what has happened in a more neutral manner (but don't choose a friend or relative who is going to "unload" negative comments about your spouse).

Initially, you will be talking to your children about you and your spouse separating (or having some problems). This often occurs (but not always) before any legal documents are set to outline things like custody and living arrangements. In questions #13 + 14, we will look further at explaining to your children any details of an actual separation or divorce settlement that directly affects them.

However you decide to tell your children, the key is that you actually do this. Your children need to know what is happening. In addition at times like this, remember your emphasis should be on comforting your children, not on them comforting you. Most kids feel completely unprepared to respond to what is being said.

In talking to your children about divorce, they need time to process what is being said. After all, your initial announcement might leave them in shock. Give careful thought to when you are going to tell them. They do not need to hear about a "cheating" spouse or other "dirty laundry" that you would like to air. If you try to place all the blame on the absent spouse, this approach might come back to haunt you. It is not helpful to your children to feel they have to take sides. In particular, ensure that your children realize that they are in no way responsible for what has happened. It is normal for some children to blame themselves for what has happened. Address this concern and make sure that your kids realize they have played no role in contributing to your marriage problems.

Most kids have an inner sense of equilibrium that motivates them to love both parents, even if one parent has been more involved in their lives than the other parent. When you criticize an absent parent, your child might end up disliking you more than the absent parent. Treat your former spouse with respect in your conversations with your children. In conducting support groups for children of divorce, one of the commonest complaints I heard from students was the discomfort that they experienced when parents "bashed" their former spouse. Kids want, and need, to be able to love both parents, and it doesn't help them when parents attempt to belittle each other.

Mary's parents separated when she was thirteen. At first, she lived with her mother. Unfortunately her mother constantly ranted about her "cheating" former husband. Six months after the separation, Mary refused to return back to her mother's after a weekend visit with her father. She said she couldn't stand to live with her mother anymore because she was sick of hearing all the crap about her father (even though he might have deserved it).

Unfortunately Mary's decision resulted in her having to change schools. A few months later, Mary grew tired of hearing her father complain about her "lazy" mother (even though they no longer lived anywhere near each other), so Mary moved back with her mother. Over the next few years, Mary moved eight times back and forth between her parents until she finally reached the age of sixteen and moved in with her boyfriend. Her boyfriend vanished after Mary became pregnant at the age of seventeen. This is not a success story; avoid criticizing your former spouse in front of your children.

When you tell your children about your separation, anticipate their questions (the next chapter will provide some typical questions that kids ask and some sample answers). Even if they don't ask any questions they will want to know where they are going to live. They will particularly want to know if they are going to have to change schools.

It is important to realize that some children have a great fear, often unexpressed, that both parents are going to abandon them. Explain to your children that you are separating from your spouse, but you are not separating from them.

It is also important to keep in mind that kids want their parents to be happy. Sometimes children will resist talking about their own concerns because they don't want to contribute to your sadness. Adults need to seek help without depending on their kids to provide this help. And children need to know that you are receiving help from a therapist or friend.

> *"I don't think anybody whose ever been divorced can tell you divorce is easy or fun or feels like anything other a tremendous failure."*
> Sharon Stone

After explaining what is happening, it is portant to listen and reflect on what your child is feeling. It is important to be silent and listen to your child's concerns and questions. As you answer any questions or comment on any concerns, provide opportunities for your children to talk about their feelings or to ask questions. Be as honest as possible without getting into the details of your actual marital problems.

5. What should I expect after I tell my children?

For most kids, within minutes of telling them about your separation they will begin to exhibit one of the stages of grieving, often either anger or denial.

Separation and divorce are a form of loss. Some people even feel that divorce is a stronger form of loss than death because death is final while the pain of a divorce, especially where children are involved, can linger for a long time. Some adults, twenty or more years after the divorce of their parents, still believe that their parents might get back together. And some adults who divorced more than twenty years ago still suffer irrational anger when they see, hear, or even think about their ex-spouse.

If your child lost his best friend, how would you respond? It's likely that you would be patient and caring, allowing your child to experience his grief. You might even take your child to a counselor who could help him deal with the loss. It's also likely that you would go out of your way to be there for your child.

Divorce has many similarities to losing a best friend, especially for a child. While a parent might be glad to be free from an ex-spouse, a child does not necessarily see things the same way. For most children of divorce, the initial loss can be staggering. The most immediate form of loss is not having two parents living together in the same house anymore. In addition to this loss, divorce generally involves significant financial changes within a family that often results in moving. When a child moves, there can be a loss of friends, loss of teachers, loss of involvement in the community, and so on. While a parent will usually keep the same job and group of friends, this is not generally true for children. While a parent might have a stable group of friends that she can talk to, most children lose this luxury when they move.

While some children might progress through the steps of grieving in a matter of weeks, in my experience it generally takes at least a year, and some experts in the field suggest that two to three years is a normal length of time to experience grieving in some form. It is also possible that after the period of grieving is over that some event or even something said might trigger a temporary relapse back into one of the stages.

6. What can I expect if my child enters the denial stage of grieving?

When we first hear about any kind of loss, we tend to deny its possibility. It is a normal reaction to loss for people to shake their heads and say, "It can't be true." Most children experience this stage of grief after leaning about the separation of their parents. This may be particularly true when there has been little overt evidence of incompatibility between the parents in front of the children. What might have been completely obvious to the parents might have been hidden from the children.

> "Denial helps us to pace our feelings of grief. There is grace in denial. It is nature's way of letting in only as much as we can handle."
> Elisabeth Kubler-Ross

Over time, children will see that the separation and resulting divorce are permanent. During this time it is important, if at all possible, to avoid giving false hopes that you will be reuniting with your former spouse. Yes, there will be some situations where this becomes a reality, but having acknowledged this, if your kids are constantly asking about you and your ex getting back together again, their grieving might be unnecessarily prolonged if you give misleading answers to such questions.

Unfortunately, this stage may be unrealistically supported through books or Hollywood movies that portray kids finding a way to reunite their parents. While this sometimes happens, the reality is that such hopes can lead to disappointment. As with any other stage of grief, the longer a child remains in this stage, the greater likelihood there is that the child might develop irrational thoughts surrounding the divorce (that can lead directly to rejecting new relationships for either parent with other adults). A new boyfriend or girlfriend for the parent may be seen as a threat to preventing mom and dad from ever getting back together again.

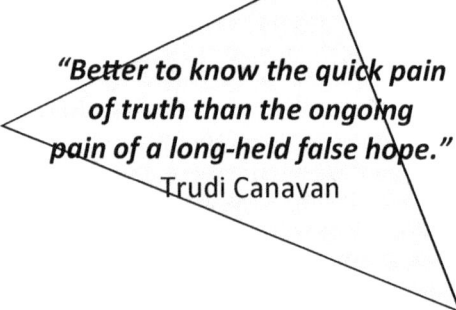

"Better to know the quick pain of truth than the ongoing pain of a long-held false hope."
—Trudi Canavan

Listening to your child's concerns and not creating false hopes can be beneficial to helping your child deal with this stage of grief. During this stage, you might find your child refusing to talk about the divorce. They might even react as though nothing has happened. They might also pull away from you, wanting to be left alone. Older children might direct more of their time to being with their friends.

You will likely experience the denial stage as well. When this happens you have to be careful that you don't get so wrapped up in your denial that you fail to be there for your children. As previously mentioned, people grieve in different ways. It is possible you could be going through a stage of anger while your children are going through a stage of denial. A professional counselor can help you and your children better understand what you are each experiencing (and provide some support for you as a parent when you are struggling with grief).

7. Should my ex and I do things together with the children?

A common question parents often ask is, "Should my parenting partner (a term which is more positive than referring to your former spouse as an "ex") and I do things together with our children (such as celebrating birthdays and Christmas)? My first response to this is that it is impossible to avoid being together to support your children. After all, if your kids are playing on a team, you and your parenting partner are going to find yourself at the same place at the same time. The same goes for school related events including parent-teacher nights. In such settings your children will benefit from you being civil to each other and from you taking a united interest in whatever they are doing.

Jose and Peter separated when their children were 6 and 8 years old. They presented a united front at sporting events and school activities (even though there came a time when new adults in their lives came along as well). They celebrated birthdays and Christmas together for a few years until it was easier to host them separately as the kids got older. In talking to the children, they loved being with both parents on special occasions when they were younger, although they both reached an age where they felt it was more comfortable not to continue this. For a time, Jose and Peter alternated years for birthday parties. One of the decisions they reached together that I think was healthy for their children was to agree on a spending limit for each child for birthdays and Christmas. This eliminated any competition between the two parenting partners in trying to "buy" their children's love. The key here is doing what is most comfortable for you and your parenting partner while also gaining some input from your children.

8. How can I deal with my child's anger?

Anger is often the most intense emotion related to grieving. Unlike death, where there might not be anyone to blame for what has happened, divorce provides a child with two people (her parents) who can be conveniently blamed (and keep in mind as well that a child often blames herself for the divorce). From my experience, for the most part, kids are going to express their anger on the parent who they see as being the most passive or simply the parent who is most convenient. Some mothers ask why their kids are so angry (even to the point of being violent) when it was their husbands who left.

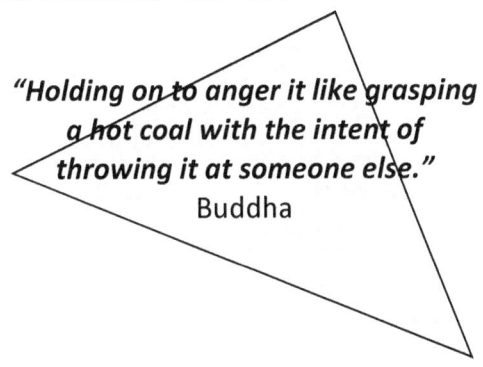

> *"Holding on to anger it like grasping a hot coal with the intent of throwing it at someone else."*
> Buddha

One woman, let's call her Sharon, divorced when her son was five. Sharon's son rarely saw his father who moved several hundred miles away (his father's choice, not his mother's). The boy vented his anger directly at his mother, sometimes even kicking and punching her. His mother permitted him to do this without telling him to stop. By the time the boy was a teenager, at times he still kicked and punched his mother, leaving deep bruises on her arms and legs. Years before, at the age of five during his grieving related to a divorce, Sharon's son learned to express his anger in an inappropriate manner. As a result, he developed habits that years later were a serious problem.

Even though anger can be a part of the grieving process, it needs to be expressed in appropriate ways. If this doesn't happen, children can develop inappropriate habits for expressing their anger that can create harmful situations for themselves and others as they grown older.

> "My parents' divorce left me with a lot of sadness and pain and acting, and especially humour, was my way of dealing with all that."
> Jennifer Aniston

In understanding anger, it has been said that the degree of anger that a person expresses is directly related to the level of inner pain he feels.

Understanding can help to ease the pain. Have you ever been angry, but simply by having someone listen carefully to your concerns, you began to feel better? When kids are able to verbalize the pain they are feeling, this can help to lessen their anger. When kids feel understood, they are less likely to lash out at someone else.

As with any other forms of grieving, there are appropriate ways to express anger. Crying is a natural response. It is okay for children (and you) to cry after experiencing divorce. Your kids should not be told that they have to be tough and resist crying, especially boys who may already subscribe to the harmful adage that men don't cry.

Physical activity is a healthy way to deal with anger. Playing on a team can be an excellent way for a child to deal with the anger of divorce. Physical activity helps to dissipate anger. According to Nathaniel Thom, a stress psychologist, "Exercise, even a single bout of it, can have a prophylactic effect" against the buildup of anger.

> *"In times of great stress or adversity, it's always best to keep busy, to plow your anger and your energy into something positive."*
> Lee Iacocca

Anger can be contagious. When your child is expressing anger towards you, avoid getting caught up in a shouting match that fuels the anger.

The manner in which you deal with your anger can provide a model for your children to help them to deal with their pain. Whether it's talking to a friend, going for a walk, going to the gym, and so on, you can be the example you want your kids to become. If you happen to be taking a class in meditation or yoga to help you deal with your anger, you could teach your kids some of these techniques.

For some children, expressing their anger in an appropriate manner is difficult to do. It might be useful for some kids to draw a picture to show how they are feeling. Another approach that works is to have kids find a song that expresses how they feel. In addition, some children write poems, stories or even keep journals related to what is happening.

Some children don't have a "feelings" vocabulary to express their pain. In support groups, I often ask the students to identify words that show how they feel. The resulting list often includes words such as angry, irritated, mad, furious, incensed, bitter, crushed, etc. Sometimes kids need to develop a vocabulary of words related to feelings before they are able to express how they are feeling.

Establishing routines can help your kids to better deal with their anger. Few people love changes in their lives. Divorce can create huge changes for children. They might end up living in one house for part of a week and then another for the other part of the week. They might be exposed to different rules and expectations in each house. They might have different meal times and even different bedtimes. And most worrisome, they might have to move to a new school and say goodbye to old friends.

Change can cause stress which can fuel anger. While you can't control what is happening in another house, you can set well defined routines in your own house which can lessen the anxiety of your children. Kids often say, after a divorce, that they enjoy being at school more than they enjoy being at home. One of the reasons for this is the clear defined structure within a school. Classes start at specified times. Lunch is the same time every day. There is consistency in all that happens. Consistent routines at home can make a positive contribution to helping your kids deal with the anger they might be experiencing. As much as possible, keep routines such as meal times and going to bed the same as they were before you got divorced.

"Outer order contributes to inner calm."
―Gretchen Rubin

As with the other stages of grieving, anger can last for days, but it can also last for months. As you observe and attempt to understand the anger your child is expressing, you should see a decrease in the intensity of the anger over time.

9. What if my child begins to make "deals" to get us back together?

When people get seriously sick, they often make a deal with God. It goes something like this, "If You heal me, I'll devote my life to being a better person." Have you ever experienced this? Sure, most of us have done something along these lines at some time or another. This is known as "bargaining" and it is another stage in the grieving process. Sometimes the bargaining is replaced by a deep yearning for the way things used to be.

It is normal for children to blame themselves for their parents' divorce. When this happens, they might become the most loving, best behaved kids in the world. In reality, what they might be thinking (subconsciously) is, "If I really try hard to be a great son, maybe my parents will get back together again." The opposite is also true. "If I become uncontrollable, maybe my parents will get back together again." In either case the child might be "bargaining" (or yearning for the way things used to be) although he does not necessarily realize what he is doing.

If a child's behavior improves after a divorce, praise the new behaviour. After all, something like doing better in school can actually help to improve your child's self-esteem. On the other hand, if the behavior is inappropriate, it needs to be confronted. It is not appropriate for a child to be doing onerous amounts of housework because she is trying to bargain with you. Similarly it is not appropriate for a child to purposely sabotage any possible success at school because she is telling you (even if this is at a subconscious level) that she will only complete her schoolwork if you and your ex-spouse get back together again. When inappropriate behavior is repeated, it can become a habit, and as adults we all know how hard it can be to break a habit, especially a bad one.

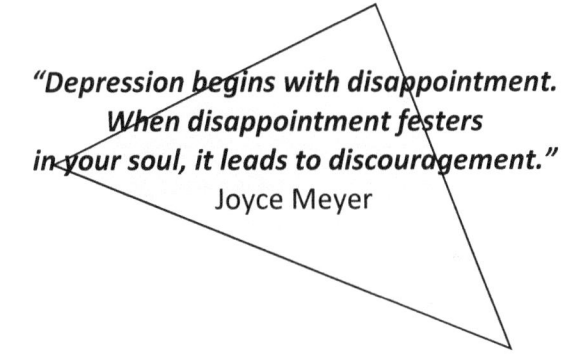

> *"Depression begins with disappointment. When disappointment festers in your soul, it leads to discouragement."*
> Joyce Meyer

Bargaining can teach your kids to manipulate others into getting what they want. In the same way that you told your kids that your divorce was not their fault, your kids need to also understand that getting back together again is not dependent on their behavior. While bargaining (or yearning) is a normal reaction to loss, it can be helpful to be aware of how your children are expressing it.

10. What should I do if my child becomes depressed?

Whenever we lose something that is meaningful to us, it is normal to become sad. This sadness can be accompanied by a sense of hopelessness which leads to various degrees of depression. Depression can prevent us from doing anything constructive: we might feel like staying in bed all day or watching hours of mindless TV, or even shutting out the world around us as we listen to music.

After a significant loss, most people stay away from work for a few days because it would be difficult for them to concentrate on their job. Most companies have a policy that allows employees to have a few days off to grieve the death of a family member. While a few days isn't always enough, it is at least something in comparison to the reality that there is often no official policy in most workplaces for time off work to mourn the death of a marriage. When adults experience divorce, they might take a few "sick" days to help them deal with the emotions and the changes they are facing.

For kids, this problem is compounded. After a divorce, they might not feel like going to school, but the longer they stay away, the more difficult it becomes to return (due to the missed work). This can become a vicious cycle of hopelessness which if not addressed can lead to ongoing problems with depression, although your kids need to have some time to mourn.

> "Someday you're gonna look back on this moment of your life as such a sweet time of grieving. You'll see that you were in mourning and your heart was broken, but your life was changing..."
> Elizabeth Gilbert

In addition to listening to your kids and hugging them, it can be helpful to get them involved in activities that are enjoyable to them. While we generally just want to do nothing when we are feeling depressed this "doing nothing" often continues to feed our feeling of being depressed. Sometimes, the best medicine - however hard it might be - is to get up and do something. It is not unusual for a divorced adult to clean her house from top to bottom, or even repaint rooms throughout the house, to focus on doing something different.

Often the best place for your child to be is back at school. As a school counselor it was normal for me to receive a call or email from a concerned parent after a separation or divorce. When this occurred, I would make contact with the student over the course of the day to see how he was doing. In this first meeting, I would inform the student that I was available to talk about any concerns related to the divorce. Generally, a day or two later, I followed up with the student to once again express my interest in helping him. Some students never pursued this help while others did, but regardless of what the student decided, I believe this contact helped the student to understand that his parent(s) cared about him (and I cared about him as well). This approach can make a difference.

Many schools have either a child care worker or social worker who has "grief counseling" training. As such, contacting the school could result in your child receiving professional help in an environment that is comfortable for her.

If your child experiences depression (often demonstrated by sadness or withdrawing from friends and family), it is important to realize that there are different degrees of depression. While sadness and hopelessness (and even related physical aches and pains) are a normal reaction to divorce, when these symptoms become extreme or do not appear to be dissipating over time, you should seek professional medical assistance for your child (especially if your child's thoughts and/or actions suggest suicide or any other form of self-harm).

Symptoms related to depression can include:

- experiencing appetite or weight changes

- feeling guilty and/or hopeless

- sleeping too much or too little

- having trouble paying attention or concentrating

- unexplained tiredness, lack of energy

- inappropriate outbursts to others

- constant crying

- feeling of loneliness

"Acceptance doesn't mean resignation, it means understanding that something is what it is and there's got to be a way to get through it."
Michael J. Fox

If your child was already receiving counseling for depression (or other mental health issues) before your divorce, it is critical that her counselor is made aware of the divorce because what is happening related to the divorce can heighten the concerns your child is already experiencing.

An important practical way to help your children

deal with depression is to help them find a way to express what they are thinking and feeling. Encourage them to talk to you, or use art, music, and/or drama to show you what they are experiencing.

Children often learn a great deal through our actions. If you are depressed, the manner in which you are attempting to deal with this can either help or hinder your child's progress in this stage of grieving. One of the most harmful approaches is for you or your children to "bottle up" what they are feeling and sink into a sea of helplessness. Talking to an empathetic friend or professional can be very helpful.

"Understanding is the first step to acceptance, and only with acceptance can there be recovery."
J.K. Rowling

11. Will my child ever accept our divorce?

The acceptance stage of grieving is sometimes described as being one of calm, not necessarily happy, but certainly not depressed. It is a stage where a person realizes that she can't change what has happened, and that there is a need to begin to think about resuming a normal way of living. Unfortunately, not everyone will reach this stage. As previously mentioned, some children (and adults) will remain fixated to some degree in one of the other stages of grieving. This fixation can last a lifetime even though in many ways the person can resume an otherwise normal life. Some kids will always harbor dreams of their parents getting back together again. Some adults will always find themselves getting angry in the presence of their former spouse.

Many people will still periodically encounter one of the stages of grief for brief periods of time (as short as a few minutes) when something (such as a picture or song) triggers a painful memory. When a child becomes fixated in one of the stages of grieving and this is affecting her relationship with others and her work at school, this is generally a signal to seek some form of help.

Most children will eventually reach the acceptance stage of grieving. They will resume their friendships with others. They will be calmer. Their personalities will be more like their pre-divorce days (and might even be improved if there is now less tension in the house). They will resume their schoolwork and other activities with energy. While this might take weeks (more likely months), it is not unusual to continue experiencing some of the grieving stages for more than a year.

In my experience as a counselor, many kids reach the acceptance stage before their parents. If you experience this, it is important that you don't drag your children back into the stage of grief that you are dealing with.

12. What should I communicate to my child's teacher(s) about the divorce?

In responding to this question, let's first of all look at some of the legal issues (and as I'm not a lawyer, you should verify what I am saying with your lawyer). In general, if a school has not received any legal notification to inform them otherwise (such as an official copy of a court order or minutes of settlement), the school will proceed to treat each parent equally. In other words, both parents will have access to report cards, attendance records and any other form of communication that a legal parent/guardian of a child might normally expect.

In some states and/or provinces, being the official custodial parent does not necessarily preclude the other parent from having access to school related information, unless there is a court order or minutes of settlement that specifically states that one parent is not to receive any communication from the school or have any contact with the children while they are at school.

Where this situation becomes more sensitive relates to the issue of which parent can actually pick up the children from the school. If there is something in your separation agreement or divorce settlement (or in a court order) that blocks one parent from contacting your children at their school, then the school needs to have this information (and they should have it in writing). Every year there are stories on the news of a parent taking his/her children unlawfully from a school. If a school doesn't have any record that there is a court order or some type of legal contract or agreement that prevents one parent from taking the children from the school, then the school can't be expected to keep this from happening.

If you have any concerns about your parenting partner having contact with your children while they are at school, you should talk to your lawyer about this and get her advice on what you need to present to the school administration to ensure that the appropriate procedures are followed.

Let's take this question beyond just the possible legal issue involved. Most parents tend to resist talking to teachers or school counselors about a divorce or separation. As one parent said to me, "I don't want any teachers to know about my family's problems."

I understand the rationale for some parents not wanting teachers and/or school counselors to know about what is happening within their family. Unfortunately, the end result of this for some kids is to begin a downward spiral in class without anyone understanding why this is happening. Such thinking also encourages kids to bury their feelings about what is happening at home. Most adults have someone to talk to about what is happening in their lives; children can often benefit from having a trusted adult at school to talk to.

Earlier in this book, I shared the story of Rosemary. Rosemary was a grade 1 student who was suffering incredible pain related to her parents' separation. At first, Rosemary's parents decided not to provide any information to the school on what was happening at home. Rosemary's self-esteem took a hard hit before her teacher was able to discover what was causing the problems at school.

Once the teacher became aware of the concerns at home, she was able to arrange for a school social worker to talk to the parents. With some counseling for the parents and Rosemary, and with some remedial help at school she began to improve her work. Before the year was over, Rosemary made significant progress in accepting her parents' separation as well as achieving the expectations for her grade level at school.

What is happening at school can help your children to better deal with divorce.

Sometimes I have received a telephone call from a parent saying, "My spouse and I have just separated.

This is a very emotional time in our home. I don't know how this is affecting my daughter at school, but I would appreciate it if you could find out how she is doing. If there is no problem, we don't want to create one, but if she is struggling we would like to arrange help right away."

If your child is suffering, consider the resources that are available within a school. A strong classroom teacher can assist your children by helping him to be successful at school. Success at school can have a direct impact on your child's self-esteem. Even when things are falling apart at home, you might be able to help offset some of this by helping your child to be successful at school. In addition, a school counselor with experience in helping kids with problems related to a divorce might just be the perfect person your child could talk to.

13. What form of custody and living arrangements are best for my children?

These are difficult questions. There are different forms of custody arrangements (which in turn can have a direct impact on living arrangements). Different countries may have different terminology so anything to do with custody should be discussed with a legal expert.

Generally legal custody refers to who makes the important decisions (such as schools or health care) for your children. Physical custody refers to who the children live with. Joint legal custody places the right and responsibility for important decisions in the hands of both parents. Sole legal custody places the right and responsibility for important decisions in the hands of one parent. Joint physical custody means that the children live with both parents (although this does not have to be a 50/50 split in time) while sole physical custody means the children will live with one parent most of the time and usually visit the other parent.

Visitation orders spell out a plan for how parents share their time with their children.

The law generally states that judges must give custody according to the "best interests" of the child. Factors that are considered in making such a decision often include:

- the age of the child

- the health of the child

- the emotional bond between the parents and child

- the ability of the parents to care for the child

- the mental and emotional health of the parents

- sibling concerns

- who was the primary care giver before the separation?

- any history of family violence or substance abuse

- the child's ties to school, home, and community

Mediators or family counselors, who are trained in understanding what is best for children, are often involved in helping to make the best decision. Parents can also discuss and lay out the framework for their custody arrangements (to be approved by the court).

> *"The courts of this country should not be the places where resolution of disputes begins. They should be the places where the disputes end after alternative methods of resolving disputes have been considered and tried."*
> Sandra Day O'Connor

Where possible (and after considering any safety concerns), children generally benefit the most when both parents remain involved in their lives. Older children (generally over the age of 12) often have direct input into living arrangements.

Where parents live within the same school district and are both able to care appropriately for their children, some parents will decide on having their children live with one parent for a week and then switch. There are a number of variations of this arrangement. While such an arrangement gives your children time with both parents (which is important), it has the disadvantage of regular moving for the children and can create additional costs with having to maintain clothing, etc. at two houses. A family counselor can be very helpful in assisting you to determine what is best for your children. Children are unique, and what works for one family might not be appropriate for another.

14. What do my kids need to know about the divorce settlement?

When most parents first separate, there is often no formal agreement on any living arrangements with the children. Sometimes parents even separate (emotionally and physically), but remain in the same house due to financial restraints. Eventually whatever informal agreements that exist between the two spouses will become more formalized. This often occurs when the adults involved realize the financial implications of what is happening (or one of the adults develops a serious relationship with someone else). This generally results in the need to divide some or all of the assets that were accumulated during the marriage. While some adults will begin to formulate an agreement together, or with the help of a mediator, it is normal for lawyers to become involved at this point (and you should have legal advice related to any form of agreement that you make).

In many cases a well designed separation agreement will become the foundation for the divorce settlement. Given the emotions of both anger and guilt that can be involved in separating, it could be very useful to obtain legal and counseling support to create a fair settlement. In counseling adults, too often I hear a father or mother say something along the lines of, "I just wanted to get the other person out of my life, so I signed whatever was suggested as quickly as possible so I could move on. Now I'm dying in debt because of the unfair agreement that I made."

A fair settlement can help both parents move forward with less resentment against each other. Over and over I hear kids saying that they wish their parents would stop fighting (sometimes more than a decade after the divorce). A fair divorce settlement can assist in preventing future arguments and be one less reason for former spouses to attack each other.

As explained at the beginning of this chapter, separation/divorce is a form of loss. As your child mourns her loss, she can become sensitive to the smallest further disruption in her life. Kids need to know the details of a separation agreement or divorce settlement that directly affect them. For example, where will they be living and when? Will they still be able to attend the same school? Who will pick them up from school and on which days? Who will be driving them to evening practices or lessons?

Where will their pets live? If at all possible in making these decisions, your kids should have some input (and this might require the help of a qualified child specialist, counselor, social worker, or family mediator).

As you begin to think about talking to your children, it is important to remember that you, or your parenting partner, might still be in the anger or denial stage of your grieving. As such, your best intentions to talk to your children together can turn into a shouting match of blame. While it is important to talk to your kids (and not prolong the uncertainty of what is happening), you need to consider your emotional state. It might be necessary to involve another person, someone neutral, in talking to your children.

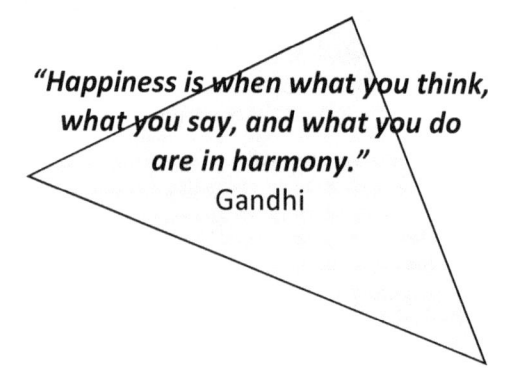

"Happiness is when what you think, what you say, and what you do are in harmony."
Gandhi

One of the keys is to remember that some pre-planning on what you are going to say is important. If you and your ex-spouse give completely different messages about what is going to happen regarding living arrangements, school, etc., this can cause significant confusion that gets added to your child's attempt to deal with their loss. Children often ask "Why do I have to be caught in the middle of the conflict when I wasn't the one who decided that my parents should get divorced?"

Considering the changes that your children are going to be facing, the least divorcing parents can do is to present a unified front in talking to their kids about what some of these changes are going to be, and to listen to their questions and concerns.

In talking to your kids about divorce, it is normal to try to "soften the blow". Be careful that you don't create false hopes of getting back together again if they are not warranted. When you do this, you might be preventing your children from experiencing the normal stages of grieving. Sometimes parents with passive personalities create problems because they avoid talking about the issues.

Kids don't need to know about any affairs or money problems that led to the divorce, and it is important that your conversations about these things should not be occurring while your kids are present (most kids can hear a long way from their bedrooms). If you want your kids to survive the divorce in a healthy manner, they don't need to know about the adult issues. Blaming an ex-spouse can be confusing to your children. They want to be able to love both parents, and blame can fuel their sense of guilt when they might otherwise be enjoying their time with the other parent. Children often have an image of each parent that is likely different than your perception. It doesn't help your children to destroy their image of their other parent. It generally makes more sense to say that you are not getting along with their other parent than to give them painful details of why you are not getting along.

It is typical for most kids to blame themselves in some way for the divorce. As you talk to your children about the divorce, emphasize that the divorce is a result of disagreements between you and your parenting partner. Kids need to be reassured that they did not cause the divorce. I have had young children tell me that their parents were getting a divorce because they wet their bed or because they didn't eat their supper. Kids can twist whatever they hear. Be very careful that you do not refer to any of your children when you might be "venting" your emotions. They might only hear a few words of what you say, but they might internalize that you are angry at them.

Kids are concerned about the well-being of their parents. They want you both to be happy. There is often some form of turbulence or unhappiness before a separation that continues into the divorce. Kids sometimes sense that you are unhappy during these times. Stressing with your children that you will be happier after the divorce can help them to feel better.

Children also need to be reassured that as parenting partners, you will continue to be their parents forever. It is normal for children to think that after parents have left each other, the next step might be for them to leave their kids. Children can feel a sense of abandonment after a divorce. Kids need to hear (and see) that you are not leaving them. They need to hear that you love them and they need to receive your hugs.

Separation agreements and divorce settlements are sometimes made when one, or even both parents, are still struggling with their own grieving. Unfortunately they are also sometimes orchestrated by lawyers who might engage in an adversarial approach. Such lawyers tend to encourage couples to focus on the worst of each other. While lawyers can help you to resolve your issues to determine what is best for your children, be careful of any lawyers that focus on feeding your anger. At a time when you might be fragile, a lawyer with an adversarial approach can fuel your desire for revenge. Not only can agreements under such circumstances prove harmful to your children, but once you and former spouse begin to attack each other through the legal process, your eventual bill can be staggering (and your distrust of each other and your anger can increase).

15. How can a mediator help us?

A family court mediator or a qualified family

counselor is a professional who can assist you in forming some aspects of your separation/divorce agreement, especially the sensitive issues involving your children.

In addition, a mediator generally charges far less than a lawyer (and often has more training when it comes to understanding the needs of your children). Most divorced couples struggle financially after a divorce. Huge lawyer bills can exacerbate this problem. Although it is estimated that approximately 90% of divorce settlements occur out of court, a lack of collaboration between you and your ex-spouse, or even between the two lawyers can become a very expensive proposition. A mediator can provide a cheaper alternative (although it is important that your lawyer reviews your agreement before you sign it).

Some law offices now have mediators who work for them. In some locations, there can be court appointed mediators. If you need to find a mediator on your own, talk to friends for recommendations. Check the internet for reviews of anyone that you are considering. It is important to realize that in some locations there are no professional requirements for someone to call himself a mediator. Ensure that the person you are working with has specific qualifications (and references). Not only can a mediator be significantly cheaper than a lawyer, but they are often trained in helping both you and your parenting partner to understand what is best for your children (and what is best for your children is often what is best for you as well). Mediation can provide positive long term benefits for you and your children. There is a tendency in mediated agreements for both parents to be more involved in the future of their children which can be very beneficial to them.

If you are involved with a mediator or child specialist to help you negotiate a fair settlement for all involved, it might also be useful to meet together with this professional at regular intervals (perhaps once or twice a year) to review how things are going. Circumstances can change (such as job commitments or school concerns or even the involvement of one of your children in an elite level of sports, music or drama). The rapport previously established by the professional who was involved in your divorce settlement can help you to more quickly resolve any future concerns that might arise. Such experts can also help you to tailor your agreement based on what is appropriate for the ages of your children. The living arrangements for a one year-old might be significantly different than that of a sixteen year-old.

In addition to helping you to develop a fairer and more workable agreement, a mediator should also be able to assist in helping you to understand what to say to your children (and in some instances it might even be appropriate to have the mediator present when you talk to your children). A mediator can talk to your children to get their input into their concerns and to help them to be a part of a fair settlement.

If you work with a mediator or counselor to establish things such as your living arrangements with the children, whatever agreement you come to should be examined by your lawyer before you sign anything. While a mediator can be a wonderful resource for some aspects of your divorce agreement, there are other considerations (especially financial) that might need the expertise of a lawyer (or a tax expert or financial consultant).

Once your agreement has become a legal document, it will take both time and money to make any future changes (and sometimes it can be very difficult to alter the original terms of an agreement without just cause), so it makes sense to cover as many aspects of your settlement as possible the first time around.

Another approach is called collaborative law which can provide a couple with a team that could include a lawyer, a financial specialist, a coach (a relations specialist) and a specially trained child specialist. This approach can help couples to negotiate a fair settlement while also being cognizant of the legalities that relate to divorce agreements. It can also provide a wider range of expertise than one professional would typically possess.

Although it is impossible to predict the future, there can be decisions made that a year or two down the road become unworkable. For example, in one divorce settlement a father had only one week of holidays each year at the time of the settlement and therefore agreed to spend just one week of vacation time with his children. The mother on the other hand was a teacher and had the complete summer off as well as school breaks. A few years later, the father had a new job which gave him four weeks of holidays. With a change of circumstances it made logical sense (as well as being fair in the eyes of the children) to make some adjustments to the vacation arrangements for the children. Unfortunately, the mother refused to make any changes to their former settlement. As far as she was concerned, the divorce settlement was etched in stone, never to be altered.

Eventually, lawyers became involved and money was wasted (and the children were exposed to more fighting) on a decision that ultimately altered the vacation arrangements. Sometimes an expert who is helping you with the settlement might be able to foresee situations like this and offer some suggestions to incorporate in the agreement to allow some future flexibility in things like living arrangements.

Underlying the details of any divorce settlement, kids need to know that both parents still love them. Yes, there can be times when one parent fails to live up to his/her responsibilities. In such situations, let the facts speak for themselves without having to editorialize. Children need to understand that mom and dad are getting divorced from each other, but they are not getting divorced from their children.

16. Isn't it hard for children to go back and forth between two homes?

Yes, this can be difficult for children, but when it works it is generally a good option because it keeps both parents involved, something that is important to most kids. This approach also helps both parents to be a part of the parenting process. When one parent feels diminished in his role as a parent, this often leads to arguing and dissension among the two parents.

The living arrangements that work for one family might not be practical for another family. It is important to consider practical realities such as transportation to and from school. The age of your children is also an important factor to consider. Older children (teenagers) tend to be more resistant to constant moving (unless they have grown up with this pattern in their lives).

There are a number of factors in helping your children to be happy with living in two homes. First of all, routines and consistency are a big part of being an effective parent. If it is your turn to have your children, then you must be on time in picking them up. The transition between the two houses needs to be as seamless as possible. If the "pickup" time is inconsistent or if the pickup results in you and your parenting partner expressing negative words, your child will quickly learn to feel anxious about changing houses. Sure, there will be occasions when a work commitment or a traffic concern will interfere with a regularly scheduled pickup, but these need to be the exception, rather than the rule.

I worked with two parents whose children were very involved in sports in the community. Their practices sometimes started within an hour of finishing school and whenever they had out-of-town games, they needed to leave immediately after school. As the father was self-employed and worked out of his house, it was easier for him to adjust to the changing schedules of his kids. His parenting partner on the other hand had a job that offered no time flexibility as well as being in a location that constantly presented challenging traffic conditions after work.

The parents agreed to a solution where the children went to the father's house every day after school (even when they were scheduled to be with their mother). If they had an early practice or game, the father fed them and took them to their activities. If not, they waited at their father's house until their mother was able to pick them up each day. This arrangement continued until the children were teenagers, at which time they walked to their mother's (during the times they were scheduled to be with her), made their own supper, and if necessary their father picked them up to take them to their practices or games. Even though the details of this arrangement were not written in their divorce agreement, the two parents adapted this flexible arrangement on their own to best meet the needs of their children.

Children require a set of clothing and personal effects at each home. While they might bring some of their favorite clothes back and forth as they change homes, it is not realistic to expect them to pack several suitcases each time they change homes. This is also an area where children need to take some responsibility. Parenting partners can quickly find themselves embroiled in an argument over a missing t-shirt or brand new lost shoes. For younger children, it would make sense for them to have a list of items that travel back and forth between houses.

> *"I just want my kids to love who they are, have happy lives and find something they want to do and make peace with that. Your job as a parent is to give your kids not only the instincts and talents to survive, but help them enjoy their lives."*
> Susan Sarandon

The real key for children to feel comfortable with changing houses is for parents to assist in making the move each time as painless as possible. While some parents ensure that their time with their children is positive, other parents go out of their way to sabotage what happens at the other house by purposely losing clothing or homework, or even bombarding their children with phone calls, text messages and emails. Technology provides a wonderful way for you and your children to keep in touch, but too much contact can be unsettling to your children. Encourage your children to enjoy their time with their other parent. Children need to feel that they have your permission to love their other parent.

17. What if my ex and I have completely different approaches in raising our children?

This is one of the most frequently asked questions I encounter, even when I'm not talking about divorce. The question goes something like this: "When my kids are with their father (or mother), they do whatever they want. They don't have to do their homework. There's no curfew for them to go to sleep. They can spend hour after hour watching TV or playing video games. And they stuff themselves with junk food. What can I do about this?"

First of all, in my experience in working with families, the perception of these situations is often much worse than the reality (but not always). If you are experiencing this, here are three possible responses:

> *i) concentrate on what you can control and let go of what you cannot*

*ii) talk to your parenting partner
about your concerns*

iii) involve a professional counselor or mediator

Let's look further at each of these choices.

i) Concentrate on what you can control and let go of what you cannot.

In Richard Niebuhr's Serenity Prayer, we read "God grant me the serenity to accept the things I cannot change; courage to change the things I can; and wisdom to know the difference."

Sometimes we lose a lot of sleep and create unnecessary stress in our lives by worrying about things that we cannot control. We can't control what happens when our kids are at the home of our parenting partner. This can present a problem when your children comment on the laxness of what is happening at their other home.

For example, your kids might tell you about the laissez-faire attitude at their other home where apparently there are no rules. When you hear this, first of all keep in mind that your children might be subconsciously saying to you, "If you guys were back together again, this wouldn't be happening." They might also be saying this to you because the children of divorce can very quickly adapt to the need to tell each parent what they think they want to hear. Another possibility is that they are still in the anger stage of grieving and they are trying to upset you because they are feeling pain.

In many ways what your kids tell you is often determined by how you react. Next time your kids offer to tell you something that is happening, or not happening, at the home of your parenting partner, be sensitive to how you react. By changing your reaction, you might change the behavior of your children. For example, if your kids frequently tell you about all the fun they are having at their other house, it might be that they are indirectly telling you that they wish you would spend some more time with them doing fun things. Or, it might even be that they are trying to tell you that they love their other parent (which is a good thing).

Some kids are encouraged to become "spies" which is not healthy for them. It makes far more sense to tell your kids you want to hear about the positives than the negatives. If you want your kids to grow up happy and successful, and overcome the pain of divorce, they need your permission to enjoy their time when they are not with you. Kids need your encouragement and acceptance to love their other parent.

Where in fact, the rules are non-existent at the home of your parenting partner, you need to be firm and consistent with the rules of your home. Consistent fair rules provide boundaries for kids that can help them to feel loved and accepted.

The main thing to consider is what you can control and what you cannot. You can control what happens in your home, but you cannot control what happens in the home of your parenting partner. Focus on what you can do, instead of stressing over what you cannot. The exception to this would be if you suspect that your children are being abused, for which you need to take action.

Some parents say that differences in the rules between two homes will confuse their kids. If you find yourself thinking this way, consider the reality that your kids experience each day at school. In any school there can be a wide variation in the behavioral expectations from class to class. Over time most kids learn to adapt to the different styles of discipline from a variety of teachers. In the same way, your kids can also adapt to the differences in the expectations that you and your parenting partner have. In fact, in continuously married homes, children are often exposed to two different styles of discipline as spouses can differ in their approach to rules in the house.

ii) Talk to your parenting partner about your concerns

Whether the home of your parenting partner is as clean as your home, or whether your parenting partner prepares the same quality of meals as you might be immaterial to the future happiness of your children. If you are going to express some concerns to your parenting partner, ensure that these are concerns that truly affect the welfare and happiness of your children.

There are some legitimate expectations that parents should attempt to keep consistent between both houses. One expectation addresses schoolwork while another addresses sleep. To these you could add behavior, especially in the area of getting along with others.

When your kids return back to your house, you should be able to determine whether they completed their homework while they were with your parenting partner. You should also be able to observe whether they have been getting enough sleep.

If your observations tell you that there are concerns on an ongoing basis, it would make sense to talk to your parenting partner about this. Yes, this could result in further conflict. Yes, you might be told to mind your own business. On the other hand, if you present your concerns without attacking the other person (focus on the specific details of your concerns), you might achieve some results that benefit your children. In voicing your concerns, don't do this in front of your children. Choose a time when they are not going to overhear the conversation. Also keep in mind that some people respond better to texts, emails, phone calls, or in person chats. Learn what works best for you and your parenting partner, and attack the problem, not the person.

It can be beneficial for parents to talk every few weeks (or even more often) about their kids. It is healthy for your kids to realize that you are both concerned. It is also healthy for your children to realize that you can talk peacefully about them. Some kids are well aware that the continued fighting is directly or indirectly related to them and this increases their pain and guilt. Some parenting partners even get together at a local coffee shop on a regular basis to talk about their children.

When you have any concerns to share, there are various ways to keep your conversation civil. Once you begin to talk about your concerns, avoid making demands and avoid verbally attacking the other person. It makes more sense to say something along the lines of, "I try to have the kids in bed by 9 each night. How do you feel about this?" If your parenting partner answers that this makes sense, you might respond by saying something along the lines of, "Could we agree that we will both try to maintain a bedtime of 9 o'clock regardless of which house they're at?" If you get a positive response from your parenting partner you have an agreement that hopefully you can both maintain. Such a routine at both houses can be very beneficial to your children. On the other hand if your parenting partner says that 9 is not suitable for him (or her), ask what is appropriate? If he says 10, could you compromise on 9:30? If you can't agree, then you might have to maintain the routines in your house while trying to ignore what is happening elsewhere unless the problem is severe enough that you need to involve a mediator to help.

In regards to homework, a strategy that can work is for your kids to have a homework book or an agenda that they carry with them each day. Any homework assignments or tests are written into this book. This approach works particularly well if teachers sign the book at the end of each class for the first few weeks. Each evening after the homework is completed, the parent checks the work and signs that it has been done. Using this type of approach, parents can help to ensure that homework is being completed, and each parent can also see what transpired during the time their child was at the other house.

iii) Involve a professional counselor or mediator

If you still have unresolved concerns after you tried the suggestions provided on the last few pages, it might be necessary to involve a professional counselor or mediator.

In many communities a good starting place might be through the child care worker, social worker or guidance counselor at the school of your children. A skilled counselor/therapist can help parenting partners to present a consistent and fair approach to establishing and maintaining routines. Such an approach can be invaluable in helping your children to move forward. Success at school can play a huge role in helping kids to improve their self-esteem at a time when they really need some help. In choosing a therapist, look for someone who has qualifications related to family counseling.

18. What if my co-parent and I can't stop fighting?

As previously mentioned, this is a major concern for children. Kids often say, "My parents told me they were getting a divorce because they weren't happy together. Now that they are divorced, they fight even more. When are they going to stop?"

Divorcing someone you once loved (and perhaps still do) can be a very emotional experience. The emotional reaction to what is happening generally increases if one person perceives the other person as having financial advantages, or when one or the other person starts dating.

It is okay to reach out for help. It is okay to talk to a counselor about what you are experiencing. It might even be necessary for you and your parenting partner to talk to a counselor together to avoid having heated arguments in front of your kids.

If you and your parenting partner are constantly fighting, consider some of the following thoughts:

- the health and well-being of your children, and their acceptance of the divorce (and the resulting living arrangements) are often directly related to your happiness and positive adjustment to what has happened

- studies have shown that children can suffer psychological harm when there is a high degree of conflict between parents

- do you want to engage in costly, time-consuming legal procedures that can destroy any possibility of you and your parenting partner ever being civil to each other again?

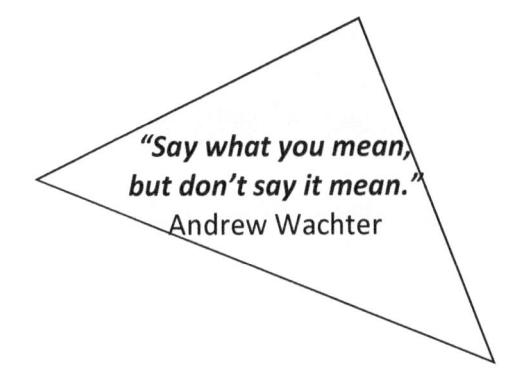

"Say what you mean, but don't say it mean."
Andrew Wachter

DIVORCE and CHILDREN

19. What should I do if my child is struggling at school?

What is happening at school can play a huge role in determining how kids feel about themselves. Children of divorce tend to deal with serious image issues. Many kids believe that they caused the divorce (especially if they hear their names mentioned when their parents are arguing). Many kids will experience feelings of hopelessness and depression. Some kids will become quiet and sullen because they have lost whatever confidence they had. These and some of the other negative consequences of divorce can have a harmful effect on what is happening at school.

"Research shows that academic achievement influences the level of self-esteem."
Ranjit Singh Malhi, Ph.D.

Research studies have shown that high self-esteem and school success generally go hand in hand. Your child's self-esteem might suffer as a result of your divorce placing her at risk for a multitude of possible problems. Helping kids to achieve at school is one positive approach to increasing their self-esteem and avoiding some of the other problems that relate to drugs, crime, bullying, and self-harm.

James Battle was one of the first researchers to look at the link between depression and self-esteem. He discovered that as depression rises, self-esteem tends to decline. As stated above, success at school can be beneficial in increasing a child's self-esteem which in turn can help him to better deal with any depression that is a normal part of grieving a loss. Self-esteem is sometimes defined as having self-confidence or the conviction that one is generally capable of achieving success.

If your child begins to experience a lack of success at school, this can compound the pain they are suffering related to divorce. Kids can begin to tell themselves that they are "not good at anything" or that they are "losers". Such self-talk over a period of time can form habitual negative thinking that can in turn sabotage any future happiness and success.

What is happening at school is often a good snapshot of how your child is responding to a divorce.

Research studies (one study analysed and summarized 95 studies that included more than 13,000 children) showed that children of divorce often did poorly academically at school and also demonstrated inappropriate behavior (acting out, being more aggressive, sometimes even bullying, or being withdrawn). In other words the research tends to support the notion that what is happening at school can be an outward reflection of the pain or difficulties a student might be experiencing related to a divorce. Therefore it makes a lot of sense to explore what is happening at school.

If your child is having difficulties at school in addition to the pain of dealing with a divorce, this can be a serious combination of problems. Resolving these issues should be a priority for you and your parenting partner.

Some kids might have already been struggling at school long before the divorce. If you see a divorce on the horizon it would make sense to get some supports in place at school before your child is facing any additional concerns. These supports could include tutoring, counseling, and remedial help.

In talking to any staff members at your child's school, it is important to stress the confidential nature of your request, and to let your child know that you are making a request for help. It can be devastating to a child for a teacher to suddenly mention the divorce without the child having any knowledge that the teacher was told about it. Most kids would like to believe that school is one place where they do not have to relive the problems that are happening at home.

If it appears that it is going to be in the best interests of your child to talk to a school counselor, it makes sense for you to talk to your son/daughter about this first. If a school counselor calls a student into her office to talk about a concern such as a divorce, the first question the student is going to ask is, "How do you know about the divorce?" The counselor isn't going to lie. If your child has not been prepared for this, your child might grow angry at both you and the counselor, and as a result resist getting help. Be honest with your kids, although this doesn't preclude an exploratory call to the school to see what services and help they can provide.

As a school counselor, once I received such a request from a parent, I asked each of the child's teachers to give me a brief overview of the child's current progress in class as well as any behavioral concerns. With younger children, your child might only have one teacher. As such, you might find it helpful to simply contact this teacher. For older children where they have a number of teachers, it makes more sense for a school counselor to coordinate the reports from the teachers.

After I received the initial reports from the teachers and shared them with the parent(s) and student, I offered to repeat this process in another few weeks. Where there were concerns, I would recommend counseling, remedial help, or some other form of assistance.

If your children are failing (or falling behind), remedial help (whether within the school or from an outside source) should be explored. For some kids, placing a focus on improving their school work can help to take their minds off the divorce. As mentioned previously, improving school work also has the additional advantage of helping a child to feel better about himself.

Sometimes after assessing what is happening at school and after talking to the student, the school counselor might recommend a family mediator, social worker or even a psychologist to provide counseling/therapy for the child and sometimes for the family. It is far better to address problems before they spiral out of control. In addition, if inappropriate behavior is being demonstrated by the student, whether at home or at school, it is important to address this before it becomes habitual.

Craig was a 32 year-old man who was still suffering from a divorce 24 years after it happened. Every time Craig was close to getting serious with a woman, he would terminate the relationship. Every time he was a step away from being promoted at work, he would quit his job. This destructive pattern was established when he was 8 years old.

At the age of 8, Craig's parents divorced. Twenty-four years later Craig still vividly recalled doing everything possible at that time to please his parents. He recalled helping out around the house. He said he became a model student at school. In the end though no matter how hard he tried, his parents were still sad. He desperately wanted to make them happy.

As time went on, Craig felt guilty about being successful at school when his parents were unhappy. Soon Craig began to sabotage his own success at school. He said that he even remembered completing some assignments and never handing them in. He also recalled pulling away from his friends.

Over time, the thoughts that were established in Craig's mind at the age of 8 became unconscious patterns that guided his life. He went from job to job, and relationship to relationship. He was afraid to commit to others because he was afraid of getting hurt again. He was hesitant to be successful because he felt guilty about this, an irrational thought he had developed 24 years ago.

There are aspects of Craig's situation that could have been have been dealt with effectively when he was 8. He could have learned that many kids feel guilty when their parents divorce. He (along with the involvement of his parents) could have learned that it was okay for him to be successful. His parents could have learned that his exemplary behavior at home and school, before he abandoned this approach, needed to be acknowledged. Craig wanted to please his parents. He wanted to feel accepted. He needed to be given permission that it was okay for him to be happy and successful. Craig could have become a happy, successful adult.

20. What is normal behavior for a child after a divorce?

From my experience, and from various research studies, kids may exhibit some of the following as a normal reaction to divorce:

- poor academic results at school
- tendency to argue more with parents
- tendency to withdraw from others
- difficulty following rules
- more frequent anger outbursts
- obvious frustration in completing schoolwork
- "acting out" behaviors
- bullying

While these forms of behavior might be classified as some of the normal responses to suffering a loss, they are not normal in terms of being acceptable. As you attempt to understand the behavior of your children, it might be useful to reread the earlier questions in this chapter related to the stages of grieving.

While it can be useful to understand the root cause of inappropriate behavior (inner pain, frustration, feeling abandoned, feeling unaccepted, etc.), this does not mean that you have to accept the behavior, especially in its extreme forms. Unacceptable behavior is unacceptable regardless of the underlying reasons for the behavior.

> "If you can control your behavior when everything around you is out of control, you can model for your children a valuable lesson in patience and understanding...and snatch an opportunity to shape a character."
> Jane Clayson Johnson

Once again, this is one area when school and home present a unified front, the results will be more significant. Stopping inappropriate behavior now prevents it from becoming a habit. In addition, stopping inappropriate behavior tells our children that we love them. Structure, routines, consistent fair rules, and expectations all contribute to a child feeling loved.

Children who feel unloved are often those who are neglected. Unfortunately, it's all too easy for divorced parents to get caught up in their emotional pain, their financial problems and even new relationships to have time for their children. Make no mistake about it; it is not easy to be an effective parent when you are struggling with your own issues. When it becomes apparent that your kids are crying out for help, perhaps this is also a signal that you need help as well.

21. What can I do if my parenting partner tries to buy our child's love?

Sometimes a parent will purchase gifts for a child of divorce to win her love. This is not a healthy practice if you are hoping that your child will grow up to be happy and successful. Purchasing gifts for a child when she is confused or sad can teach her to continue to act this way when they want something else.

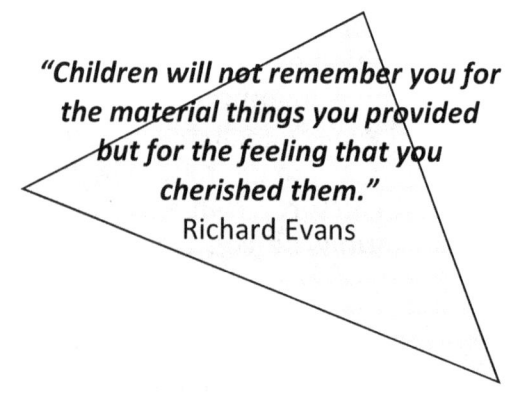

> *"Children will not remember you for the material things you provided but for the feeling that you cherished them."*
> Richard Evans

Random gifts from one parent can create a conflict with the other parent. Regardless of the real motive, a series of gifts can be seen as an attempt to bribe a child for her love. Kids know when they are being bribed, and while they often gladly accept the bribes, they generally lose respect for the person who is giving them.

While giving unexpected gifts to children can confuse them, some kids will quickly learn that they can play up their pain to gain further rewards. Some kids will learn that they will be rewarded for playing the helpless victim. There are a significant number of parents (and not just those who have been divorced) who wished they had told their children that they couldn't go through life expecting free handouts. Perhaps you know some parents who are still giving their adult children "handouts" because they never learned to say no to them when they were children.

Sometimes in these situations, the gift giving can spiral out of control with one parent trying to outdo the other. This can result in increased conflict and can prevent the child from accepting the divorce and moving on with his life.

An approach to handling this type of situation that has worked for a number of parents is to find some agreement on gift giving limits for birthdays and occasions such as Christmas. Some kids tend to "milk" their parents on these occasions. When they know the limits they can then ask for appropriate gifts within these limits.

The concern about gift giving can apply to other

situations as well. One of the more difficult situations when kids live between two houses involves pets. A child receives a dog at one house, but not the other. As a result, when the child is at the other house in addition to missing her parent, she is now missing her pet. I'm not saying that families shouldn't have pets (in fact, pets can often be a source of comfort for your kids when they are experiencing difficult times), but it would make more sense, if possible, for the child to perceive that the pet is a family pet that gets to travel with your child between the two houses. Obviously this would work better with smaller pets such as rabbits, guinea pigs, hamsters, etc.

Unfortunately material comforts between two houses aren't always going to be equal. As parents, we need to do the best we can with what we've got. As mentioned in another answer, there are some things we can control and some things that we can't; our well-being often depends on knowing the difference.

One of the most sensitive issues related to divorce, and in my experience one of the major sources of continuing conflict relates to child support. Child support can become a source of conflict for both the person paying the support and the receiver.

For the receiver, late payments or non-existent payments can cause anxiety, stress and sometimes even a lack of providing the basic necessities (food, clothing, and shelter) for your children. In some jurisdictions, support payments have now become a form of automatic pay deduction from the person who is paying which can help to eliminate the need for the receiving person to be "chasing" the other person for the support payments.

For the person paying, support payments can cause both emotional and financial pain, especially if the agreement is not perceived as being fair or the receiving parent flaunts the misuse of the support payments by enjoying exotic trips and a closet full of new clothes while the kids go without. When the support payments come from the parent who has what are perceived to be unequal visitation rights, this can fuel intense anger. As one parent said to me, "It is a crime that I have to pay my ex-spouse an inordinate amount of money each month when I barely get to see my kids." The two parenting partners involved in this situation were still fighting like cats and dogs ten years after their divorce, and their children were the real losers in this.

22. Should I be concerned if my child displays little reaction to the divorce?

Yes, especially if your child suddenly becomes sullen and withdrawn which is a visible shift from the way he normally behaves. Too often, kids who are silent are ignored. While denial is one of the stages of grieving, you need to be sensitive to a child who displays a prolonged period (weeks and months) of not even reacting to the divorce. Children who outwardly express their anger and displeasure at the divorce often get all the attention. Just because a child is quiet does not necessarily mean that he has accepted the divorce. There is an old saying that "still waters run deep".

Although children should certainly be given the space and time to grieve, none-the-less we need to monitor their behavior. If an overt child becomes an introverted child overnight, it could be beneficial to explore what is happening at school. If the child is still outgoing at school, it might just be that she is afraid to say the wrong thing at home so she is keeping quiet. On the other hand, if her behavior at school has also changed dramatically, then it might be time for some form of intervention.

Moving through the stages of grief generally requires a person to talk about his feelings with someone else. When kids don't have this opportunity, their pain can lead to depression and a general feeling of hopelessness. These feelings can lead to a lack of success at school and in some cases they can lead to more serious mental and physical health problems.

Encourage your kids to talk, and equally as important, open your ears to listen.

23. When is it okay to start dating again?

In many divorce situations the dating has already started for at least one parent before the actual divorce. The result of this is that the other parent often feels rejected. What better way to feel good again than to begin dating. While this might make logical (and emotional) sense from the eyes of an adult, it can be fraught with dangers for a child. In considering what is best for you, it is also important to consider the needs of your child who might already be concerned about you leaving him. Dating can play into this concern.

> "At the end of the day, the most overwhelming key to a child's success is the positive involvement of parents."
> —Jane D. Hull

In addition, most experts agree that it takes somewhere between one to three years before an adult is emotionally prepared to pursue another relationship. The key here is understanding when you are emotionally ready to be involved in a relationship, and when your children are ready to accept this.

There are various tests and assessment tools that professionals use to assess a person's level of risk for experiencing depression or some other form of illness. In general terms, the more changes that occur in a short period of time (let's say one year) places a person at risk of suffering greater anxiety and stress which can lead to an illness (or to making poor choices). It is generally believed that the greatest trauma a person can suffer is the death of a close friend or family member, and next might be divorce. Also near the top of the list are things like a serious illness (or accident), moving, changing jobs/schools, financial problems, new relationships, etc.

Perhaps as you read the last sentence in the previous paragraph you could already see that your children might have experienced several of these difficult life changing events in a relatively short period of time.

Dating, especially during the first few weeks following a divorce (or separation), can cause significant stress for your kids. Most children initially say they don't want another mother or father (which they think will result from your dating). A new adult in the life of either parent can cause anger and confusion. At a time when children need support from their parents, dating can result in your kids feeling abandoned if it happens too soon after your divorce, or if it prevents you from having quality time with your children.

While dating can play a role in helping an adult to successfully deal with a divorce, this is an area where the needs of your children have to be considered. At this critical time, your children need to know that they are a priority for you. After a period of time, dating can be a positive thing as your kids see that you are moving on with your life.

When you do start dating, it's advisable to let your kids know what is happening, but don't be in a rush to bring every date back to your house. Don't attempting to force another adult into the lives of your children. Let things unfold slowly and without intrusion.

Often children worry about the parent they are not currently with. If your children know you are spending positive time with friends this can help them to stop worrying about you. It can also show them that it is okay to be happy.

Take your time before introducing whoever you are dating to your kids. You don't have to give the minute-by-minute details of what you do on any dates, although for the most part your children might find it interesting to know where you went. Avoid boasting about your date which could make your children feel as though they no longer matter (at a time when they are already concerned about their relationship with their parents).

24. How can we best help our children cope with the divorce?

While the answer to this question is really the theme of this book, here are two concise answers that I hope summarize much of this book.

Kids need to feel accepted and understood. More than ever, your children need some consistent quality time with you on a regular basis. In addition, they need you to focus on understanding their point of view, rather than trying to convince them of your viewpoint. You don't have to agree with what they are saying, but understanding what they are saying is important to them. When your children feel loved and accepted, this can go a very long way to helping them to survive your divorce in a positive manner.

> *"With everything that has happened to you, you can either feel sorry for yourself or treat what has happened as a gift. Everything is either an opportunity to grow or an obstacle to keep you from growing. You get to choose."*
> Dr. Wayne W. Dyer

Secondly, kids tend to imitate what they see. If you are constantly angry and/or sad, or complaining, your kids will tend to model your negativity. On the other hand if you are moving on a deliberate path towards happiness and your own success, your example can speak volumes to your children. Be the change you want your kids to become.

25. Should I be concerned if my child starts to parent me?

While there is a tendency for most adults to laugh when they hear this question, the reality is that some children take on the role of being a parent in their house. Children can be great listeners, often far better than some adults. Most children desperately want to see you happy so if this means cooking the meals, organizing your life, and/or listening at length to your personal problems, some of them will gladly and effectively do this.

In support group sessions, students often complain about listening to their parents' problems and shouldering increased responsibilities around the house. Your children need to be children; if you need someone to share your grief with, talk to a friend or a therapist, but don't unload your problems on your children.

As has already been mentioned, children worry about their parents. They worry about your happiness. They worry about your relationships with others. They worry about the things that upset you. You will feed this anxiety if you unload your adult problems and concerns on them.

While a divorce can create a stronger bond between a parent and child, it is very important to remember that your kids need to spend time being children, spending time with their friends and doing things that are appropriate to their age group.

If you find your children beginning to look after you, this is a sign that you need to take control of your life. As mentioned throughout this book, the manner in which you handle the divorce sets an example for your children to follow. You might very well ask, "What are my children learning from me?"

26. Are there any benefits children gain from a divorce?

It often appears that there are more problems associated with divorce than there are benefits. From my experience in working with children, although I have witnessed the problems, I have also seen some benefits for kids especially when parenting partners work together to assist their children.

As an example, it takes great organization skills to move from one house to another (often during the same week) and remember everything from homework to personal items. Children of divorce get weekly practice in organizing and taking on more responsibilities.

Living in two houses, with possibly different rules and expectations, and with the addition of other adults and maybe even other children, forces kids to learn new skills in reading people and communicating with them. While some kids struggle with this, others can develop strong communication skills that will be an asset to them throughout their lives. In addition, the presence of other people can sometimes enrich the learning and skill development of children.

Living in two houses often presents a greater number of potential conflicts. When the parents involved use appropriate conflict resolution skills, children can learn from their parents, and in some cases they will have the opportunity to practice these skills in presenting their own thoughts on issues that might appear in a two-household family.

A basic tenet of divorce is that two adults who have been unhappy and unfulfilled in a relationship can change their lives and become happier and more fulfilled people. When this actually happens, your children can certainly benefit from the new you. Divorce can also provide an opportunity for you to show your kids how to overcome obstacles in achieving happiness and success.

When kids live in an environment where "penny pinching" is often a reality (as in divorce), they often develop a better appreciation of money and can learn techniques related to budgeting.

Sometimes, after a divorce, parents become more involved with their children. There is often more of an emphasis on having quality time together. Some kids say, "When my parents were married, they were always working; now that they are divorced we actually spend some fun time together."

Another benefit that some kids gain from divorce is learning to be more independent. Kids might suddenly find themselves making their own lunches or doing their own laundry. While there is a limit to the number of new responsibilities a child should be given, the reality in the end is that as kids help out a little more around the house, this can help them to develop a better sense of responsibility and independence.

27. Will I ever be able to get on with my life?

Being a parent is forever. Parenting can bring joy and it can also bring heartbreak. Even when two parents have a harmonious marriage, free from divorce, there are still times of conflict and pain. Being a parent can be difficult. Divorce can compound the difficulties of parenting, although it can also ease some of the past problems of living with someone who was a source of conflict.

As mentioned at the beginning of this chapter, divorce is a form of loss that results in grieving. Grieving takes time. How long you might ask? Unlike death, where the person you loved is gone, in divorce the person you lost is still present. This can increase the length of time in the grieving process. Some experts would say that it can take 2 - 3 years to move through the grieving process. My experience in counseling would suggest that most people can move on in less time than this. The amount of time it takes you to get on with your life often depends on resolving practical matters (such as financial concerns and living arrangements for your children). The sooner you have a fair legal settlement, the sooner you can move forward. For most people, it is the confusion of not knowing that is more crippling than dealing with the actual facts of a divorce settlement.

> *"Believe in yourself and all that you are. Know that there is something inside you that is greater than any obstacle."*
> Christian D. Larson

Victor Frankl, a survivor of the Nazi concentration camps and the author of *Man's Search for Meaning*, said that, "When we are no longer able to change a situation, we are challenged to change ourselves." There are some aspects of divorce that you can't change or control. When you accept these potential concerns, and begin to look at changing your own attitude to create a better life for yourself (and your children), you can begin to get on with your life. You can't change other people, but you can change your attitude towards others, and you can definitely change your mindset towards taking control of your own life, directing you towards a happier state of mind.

28. How should I introduce a new love interest to my children?

While on one hand your children will be interested in who you are dating, on the other they will likely feel threatened by this person. In support groups, I often hear kids of all ages say that they don't want another parent. Every time you date someone, this person is a potential partner for you (and the potential to become a step parent for your children).

In my experience I believe that one of the number one causes of new relationships falling apart relates to problems with children accepting the new adult or this person accepting the children. Obviously the problems can be compounded when both adults have children. If you are serious about the relationship and you are serious about your children (and you are also serious about your own happiness), take your time in introducing anyone new to your children. A slow approach is far better than having the person you are dating suddenly moving in with you.

> "You have to take things slowly. Just because you love someone doesn't mean that you're going to automatically love their children. All relationships take time to grow and develop. Be willing to give everyone the time and space that they need. It will come."
> Kelly LeFurgey

There are a few approaches that you can consider in introducing your children to the person you are dating (and also keep in mind that this person might also be anxious about meeting your kids). From the standpoint of your children, it might be useful to introduce the new person at your house. Your kids will feel more comfortable on their home turf. The first meeting could be brief and informal. If your children are younger, you might play a game together. If they are older, you shouldn't expect that they will spend any more time with your friend than they would normally spend with you.

Another approach would be to involve the person you are dating in an activity (such as bowling) that you might normally do with your children. Once again, there is a comfort level for your children with this approach and they won't suddenly feel that you and your new friend are trying to win their favor by doing something more exotic. Many kids feel they are cheating on their other parent when they allow themselves to have fun with someone new who you are dating.

One of the best ways to help your children to accept someone you are dating is to be positive when they talk about their other parent dating. When they talk about a new adult in their lives, if you are jealous or hostile, they will believe that dating is wrong, and when it becomes your turn to introduce someone you are dating, your children might react in the same way that you reacted when you heard about their other parent dating.

Another approach that often works related to dating is the involvement of friends or relatives who your children are familiar with. When your children see people they respect accepting the person who you are dating, this can help them to accept this person as well. In addition, a group approach permits your kids to keep some distance from this new person if they want as they can interact with your other friends.

However you handle dating and the introduction of a new person into the lives of your children, be careful what you say to your children. One woman I worked with told me that she promised her children she would never get married until they had moved out of the house and gone to college. When she met someone she wanted to marry long before her kids were going to be heading off to college, they reminded her of her earlier promise to them.

Most experts agree that you do not need to expose your children to the people you are dating if these are casual dating relationships. Your children have just suffered a form of loss related to your divorce, so introducing them to someone new who you are dating can be harmful to them if this relationship breaks up quickly and then you begin to date someone else. If your children develop a relationship with someone you are dating, and then this falls apart they will have then suffered another loss. Too many losses can prevent them from forming lasting relationships with others because they will be afraid of getting hurt.

29. What if my children don't like the person I'm dating?

In the initial stages of your relationship with someone else, it's not unusual for your children to dislike this person. If this happens, you will likely feel caught in between the desires of your children and your own desires for an adult relationship. This kind of concern helps to point out the need to take it slowly in a new relationship and in introducing this person to your children. Children have the right to feel safe and comfortable in their home (although you also have the right to be happy in a relationship with another adult). As a parent, you are responsible for respecting and maintaining this right, although there can sometimes be a fine line between respecting this right and allowing your kids to "run" your life.

My recommendation is not to force things or move too quickly. If your new relationship is not accepted by your children, there is also the danger that this relationship might fall apart if this other person feels rejected by your children. In my experience, it takes a special person (or someone who is insensitive to kids) to want to continue a relationship when rejected initially by the children involved.

If your children don't like the person you are dating, talk to them and listen to their concerns. When they feel understood, this can help them to change their perception of the situation. In addition, your children might offer some insights about the person you hadn't considered, and even offer some insights about some things you might all do together to begin to feel more comfortable.

One of the most frequent complaints I hear from parents as I conduct workshops is the amount of time that their children spend on cell phones and computers. Similarly, one of the most frequent complaints I hear from kids (from all families, not just those from a divorce) is the amount of time their parents spend on their cell phones and computers. If your evening is spent communicating with the new love in your life, your kids might resent this person long before they ever meet him or her in person. Quality time with your children (see question #31) can assure them of your love, and when they know for certain that you love them, they will be more accepting when you introduce another person to them. Remember that for many kids their greatest fear is that you are going to leave them for someone else.

30. What role should a step parent play?

Issues concerning step parents are one of the most sensitive problems for children. Part of the problem is the negative manner in which step parents are presented in stories (think Cinderella, although there are a multitude of other books and movies that create a bad image for step parents). Another part of the problem is the loyalty that children generally feel to their biological parents. Personally, I think it would be helpful to move away from the term "step parent". Perhaps, a term such as parenting partner would be better. There are some children who simply refer to the new person as a friend without having to give them the step parent label. And some kids will feel comfortable calling the new person mom or dad, or by his/her actual name. Your children should feel free to choose the term that is most comfortable for them. There are no set rules for addressing step parents.

> *"One of the most important lessons our children have learned from our divorces is that some things in life can come to an end, but that's OK because something new is manifested. In our case, it's a blended family that has respect, love, trust, authenticity and a sense of fun."*
> Jennifer Kessler

I remember one boy who was 10 when his parents divorced. During the year following the divorce, his mother dated half-a-dozen guys, all who the boy fought with. A year later when his mother finally settled down with one guy, her son once again fought openly against the man. When his mother married this man a year later, the boy referred to him as his evil stepfather (for no rationale reason). A year later, the boy began to call his stepfather John (which was his first name). Fast forward another ten years, and the boy who is now in his twenties calls this man "dad". Patience (and quality relationships) can contribute to positive changes.

The following provide some guidelines for step parents:

- never bad-mouth either of the biological parents

- in discipline matters, support the biological parent(s), but be careful not to try to take over this role (especially with teenagers)

- be a role model, someone who supports both the biological parents and the children

- be fair, don't play favorites (this is particularly important if you are bringing other children into this new blended family)

- respect and encourage special times

- don't attempt to replace a biological parent

- it takes time to build relationships, don't rush things

- respect the privacy of the children

- don't hesitate to ask your partner "What do you want me to do?"

- don't try to compete with either biological parent

- respect family traditions even if they are different than yours

- allow the children to talk about their memories and their time with their other biological parent

- give the children permission to enjoy their time with the other parent

"Too often we underestimate the power of a touch, a smile, a kind word, a listening ear, a compliment, or the smallest act of caring, all of which have the potential to turn a life around."
Leo Buscaglia

When your children see the new person in your life bringing out the best in you, they are more likely to respond in a positive way to this person. Children want their parents to be happy and often feel that divorce forces them into the role of making their parents happy. If you find someone who supports you, encourages you, brings out the best in you, and makes you happy, your children will be better able to get on with their own lives (and will have a new wonderful role model).

Discipline concerns often cause the greatest problems for blended families (and I base this observation on the frequency and intensity of questions related to discipline that are asked in my workshops). I once conducted an evening workshop on discipline in a large community gymnasium in the middle of a powerful January snowstorm. The gymnasium was packed with a standing room only crowd. This wasn't a testament to my speaking ability; it was rather an acknowledgment of the problem of discipline. As a result of this evening, I wrote the book *Discipline Without Stress*. As parents we all need help to bring out the best in our children and to create happy homes where harmony and respect are the norm.

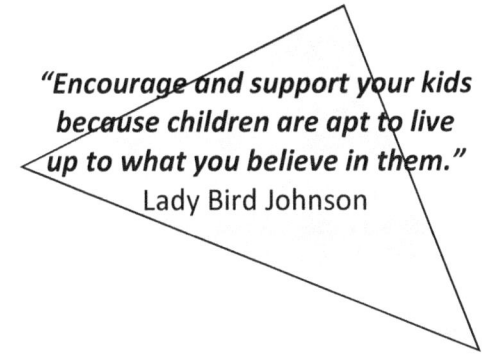

> "Encourage and support your kids because children are apt to live up to what you believe in them."
> Lady Bird Johnson

In addition to inappropriate behavior, financial concerns are a cause of problems for most families. This is particularly true in blended families where there might appear to be an inequality in what people have (and what people are able to afford). Children do not need to be burdened with your financial problems, but they need to understand the importance of budgeting in helping you to meet your financial obligations.

31. How can I show my love to my children?

Carol was thirteen when her parents divorced. Her father left for another woman. Not only did she resent her father for hurting her mother, she had little in common with her father. He was obsessed with sports while she was in love with music and dance. They were like polar opposites. Time at her father's house was painful for her, and she readily admitted that she created hell for her father's new wife and him whenever she was there.

I asked Carol what her father could do to demonstrate his love for her. After all, he had provided a good home in a nice part of town. He regularly made substantial support payments to his ex-wife so she could also enjoy an equal standard of living. He ensured he never had a work conflict when Carol was going to be with him. So what was it that Carol wanted before she would be more civil to him? Her answer was simple: she wanted some quality one-to-one time with her father.

When I pursued this further she said she would love to just sit down and play a board game or card game with him. Although they sometimes watched

TV together, she did not consider this quality time. In addition, she said that although he was always asking about school, he had no idea which courses she had and the names of her teachers. She also said he didn't know anything about any of her friends or her future plans.

Fortunately Carol was assertive enough to talk to her father about her concerns. One of the things they started to do was play Scrabble together. Soon they set aside one night a week as their Scrabble night. In talking to Carol, it was amazing how this simple activity made such a difference for her and her father. As they enjoyed this time together, they soon found themselves talking and having greater respect for each other. And a month or so later, her stepmother got involved in the Scrabble games as well which helped to create a more positive relationship between Carol and her.

> "Play helps build a warm relationship between family members and to create a bank of positive feelings and experiences that can be drawn upon in times of conflict."
> Carolyn Webster-Stratton

Time and time again, I have seen children and parents bond over playing a game together. This approach creates an enjoyable time for everyone involved and helps to solidify the bond between family members. When you set aside a specific time each week for this, it becomes something for everyone to look forward to. For younger children, you might find yourself playing a game almost every night, while for teenagers once or twice a week might be sufficient.

While spending quality time with your kids is important, it is also important for them to be encouraged to spend some time by themselves and with their friends.

"When you really listen to another person from their point of view, and reflect back to them that understanding, it's like giving them emotional oxygen."
Stephen Covey

One of the most effective ways to demonstrate your love for your children is to listen to them when they are talking to you. Most kids, at some point in their lives, talk nonstop to their parents. Unfortunately when they feel their parents are not listening, over time they stop talking. A common complaint I often hear from parents is, "Why don't my kids talk to me anymore?" The reason is often because your children think you are not listening. It might be that you are caught up in work or your own problems. It might also be because when you think you are listening, you might actually be doing most of the talking. Effective listening requires focusing on only one thing: the person speaking.

In some homes, there is friction when it is time for the children to go to bed. Many parents resolve this concern by having clear, consistent, routines related to going to bed. Once these routines become a habit, there is less arguing about bedtime. For many parents, one of the routines that works effectively is to have a story at bedtime. Younger children often enjoy listening to their parents reading to them. Older children will often accept a parent sitting in their room reading as well, even if you and your teen are reading different books. Once this routine is established, it creates a quiet time that often leads to your child talking. Taking the time to listen to whatever your child is telling you can make a huge difference in showing your children that you love them. This is a key time to shut off your cell phone and to delay whatever you might be rushing to get to next.

Routines are a practical way to show your children that you care about them.

32. What are some do's and don'ts related to helping my children successfully deal with divorce?

Although the answers to the other questions in this chapter deal with this question, you might appreciate having some succinct tips to keep in mind which provide a summary of the previous answers. The following provide 10 tips related to the do's and don'ts of helping your children.

10 THINGS TO DO

1. Make it very clear that you love your children, not just through your words but through your actions.

2. Listen to your children.

3. Be flexible in your living arrangements when your children have an opportunity to do something special with their other parent.

4. Give your children permission to love their other parent.

5. Allow your kids to express their frustrations and concerns.

6. Be honest about what is happening (without blaming).

7. Let your child know that your divorce is not their fault.

8. Be physically and mentally there for your children.

9. Be a role model. Take positive action to seek a better life for yourself.

10. Maintain standards and expectations for your children related to their behavior and school work.

10 DON'TS

1. Don't fight with your parenting partner in front of your kids.

2. Don't expect your kids to take sides.

3. Don't make the transition between homes an awkward time.

4. Don't badmouth your parenting partner.

5. Don't ignore inappropriate behavior from your children.

6. Don't let work and new relationships take away quality time with your kids.

7. Don't tell your children every detail of your worries, whether they are financial or your anger at your parenting partner.

8. Don't expect your kids to instantly love the person you are dating.

9. Don't let your children become your parent.

10. Don't try to buy your children's love.

> *"There are things in my life that are hard to reconcile, like divorce. Sometimes it is very difficult to make sense of how it could possibly happen. Laying blame is so easy. I don't have time for hate or negativity in my life. There's no room for it."*
> Reese Witherspoon

*"Divorce is a time of change.
It really rocks the foundation
of most people's lives. When
we have our heart broken or
our dreams taken away from us,
it is a time of growth and change."*
Debbie Ford

DIVORCE and CHILDREN

"If I had my child to raise all over again, I'd build self-esteem first and the house later. I'd finger-paint more, and point the finger less. I would do less correcting and more connecting. I'd take my eyes off my watch, and watch with my eyes. I'd take more hikes and fly more kites. I'd stop playing serious, and seriously play. I would run through more fields and gaze at more stars. I'd do more hugging and less tugging."
Diane Loomans

- 4 -
Questions That Kids Would Like to Ask Their Parents

One of the questions I sometimes ask students is, "What would you like to ask your parents about their divorce?" Most students have a wide range of questions that they would like to ask their parents, but they often feel uncomfortable doing so. Part of the reason for this is that they perceive that their parents are angry and/or sad and they worry about asking a question that might cause them to vent their anger or result in further sadness.

This chapter looks at the questions children and teenagers have most frequently asked me as a counselor. Hopefully by looking at the questions and considering some possible answers, this will help you to better understand what your children are experiencing. The questions might also help you to better understand some topics you might need to talk about with your kids. In looking at the answers to these questions, there will be some overlap as the underlying intent behind some of the questions is often similar.

1. Why did you get a divorce?

As you talk to your children about getting a divorce the answer to this question becomes a key part of helping them to understand the changes that are occurring in your family. This is not an opportunity for either parent to slam the other parent. Your kids do not need to know the details of what happened; what they need to know is that you were unhappy together. They need to know that in your eyes divorce is a solution to an unhappy and unfulfilling relationship. You might use an analogy that your kids might have experienced such as, "Sometimes we change our friends." In responding to this question, less is often better than more.

It might be useful to explain to your children the difference between separating and divorcing. In some locations there is a period of time a person must wait before filing for divorce. Having the correct information could be useful in talking about a divorce with your children (and helpful to you as well).

If one parent has had an affair, the other parent is likely feeling a great deal of hurt, humiliation, and rejection. In such a situation, to sit there and tell your children that you are no longer happy together is an understatement. It will be at moments like this that you must remind yourself that you are attempting to help your children deal with the divorce in a healthy manner. It is at a moment like this that you will need to remind yourself that your parenting partner will always be your child's parent. While adults might fall out of love with each other, parents do not fall out of love with their children.

Another reason to avoid talking about personal things such as affairs or financial problems is that these concerns are often more complicated than they first appear. One parent might accuse the other of having an affair which caused irreparable harm to the marriage. On the other hand, the parent who had the affair might accuse the other person of being controlling and/or physically unresponsive. This is a dialogue that could become ugly. I can't imagine any value for your children to be exposed to such an argument. No matter how black and white a problem might seem to one parent, the other parent (especially if he or she feels that he/she is being exclusively blamed for the divorce) can spin a very different story. The end result can be incredibly confusing to your children, and might result in your kids rejecting one parent (or even both) which can be harmful to their future happiness.

"If you spend your time hoping someone will suffer the consequences for what they did to your heart, then you're allowing them to hurt you a second time in your mind."
Shannon L. Alder

DIVORCE and CHILDREN

If your kids are older, they might very well know about any affairs or other problems that have occurred that have contributed to your marriage breakdown. Some kids are much more aware of what goes on in a marriage than we realize. In such a situation, if your children add their comments to what really happened, do your best to focus on your desire to move on and not dwell on what has happened in the past. Take the high road and stress that both adults will still be involved in parenting.

In situations where your kids know the truth about what happened and as a result refuse to see their other parent, give them some time to come around. Kids can benefit from being involved with both parents. While it might give you some satisfaction to see your kids rejecting their other parent, research tells us that in such a situation the other parent might pull away from her kids causing them to suffer guilt and grief for many years. The sense of longing that some kids develop can become so great that when they get older they might suddenly pack up and move to be with the parent who has been absent from their lives even though you have been the constant, loving parent.

Research shows that kids generally need at least one parent with strong parenting skills to help them overcome any problems associated with divorce. Part of being that positive parent is encouraging your kids to have a meaningful relationship with the other parent. Live your life so that when your kids think of love and fairness, they will think of you.

As you answer this question, your kids might really be asking, "Are you going to leave me (or is my other parent going to leave me)? As you answer the "why you got divorced" question, ensure that you also reassure your children that their two parents are getting divorced, but neither parent is divorcing them. Although you might no longer love your former spouse, you will always love your children.

2. Why don't you love daddy (or mommy) anymore?

In considering your answer to this question, your child might also be asking, "Are you going to stop loving me?" Another hidden question your child might be asking here is, "What did I do wrong to cause this?" In answering the initial question, consider responding to the other two questions even though your child didn't directly ask them.

Reassure your child that both parents will always love him and that he didn't do anything wrong. It might be useful to ask your child what he thinks about what has happened. Sometimes kids develop irrational thoughts about divorce. For example, one five year-old told me that her parents were getting a divorce because she didn't pick up her clothes off the floor in her room (and she also believed that if she kept her room spotless, her parents would get back together again).

Don't mislead your children and tell them that you will always love their other parent if this is not really true. This could create false hopes of reuniting. It might be better to say that you hope you will always be good friends with your former spouse. Children do not need to know the explicit details of what went wrong in your marriage, but you could explain that sometimes adults in a relationship lose their happiness with each other. You might say something along the lines of, "We have grown apart and as a result we don't want to live together anymore." And don't forget, "But we will always love you."

3. Why can't I see my other parent more often?

Research related to divorce tells us that 2 - 3 years following a divorce that approximately 18 - 25% of children have no contact with their fathers. Research studies have also clearly shown that when non-custodial fathers are involved in actively parenting (which includes factors such as providing emotional support, praising accomplishments, disciplining inappropriate behavior, and supporting schoolwork and other activities), their children do much better at school and in every other measure of healthy adjustment. The information here could also apply to women who have limited access or contact with their children after a divorce.

It might be necessary for one parent to encourage the other to be more involved. For a parent who only sees his children once or twice a week, it can be difficult to maintain contact. For some parents, it is easier to let go and try to start a new life somewhere else. This underlines the importance of considering a divorce settlement that encourages the future involvement of both parents.

Ken, a parent of two children, told me that he reached the point where it became too painful to see his children anymore. Regardless of how hard he tried, they were resistant to come with him when he picked them up. Once they were back at his house, they constantly texted and contacted their mother, counting down the minutes until they were back with her. After meeting with Ken's parenting partner, it quickly became obvious that she was vindictive and blamed an affair that Ken had for the marriage breakup. In her words, "Ken should suffer." Unfortunately, not only did Ken suffer, but his children suffered as well. They were taught to hate and mistrust their father. Unfortunately the day came when it was easier for Ken to move far away. After this happened, the kids turned on their mother. Years later, I met one of the kids who was now an adult. She said that the pain of the divorce almost two decades ago still caused problems for her. She (and her sibling) no longer had any contact with either parent. While her mother might have claimed a victory in getting rid of the father, in the end the children got rid of both parents.

In one research study with college students who had experienced divorce as children, the findings concluded that those who lived in sole-custody situations (living exclusively with one parent) reported more painful memories and feelings of loss than those who had lived in situations where their parents were both involved in parenting and where they lived in each parental home on a regular basis.

If your child is asking about spending more time with his other parent, is there something you can do to allow this to happen? Although children should not dictate the terms of where they live and then constantly revise these terms based on their perception (or sense of guilt) of what is happening at the other house, it can be important to listen to a child's concerns about living arrangements. A few days here or there, or a few hours after school with the other parent might help to strengthen the bond between the parent and child, and help to show whether there needs to be more changes to the living arrangements. This can be a good thing. If in the end, this results in a need to make some permanent changes to the living arrangements, these decisions can be made on what is in the best interest of the child rather than being based on anger and revenge.

As a divorced parent there might be times when you have to revisit your divorce settlement and make some changes that reflect the evolving nature of the relationships you and your parenting partner have with your kids, as well as their evolving need to spend more time with their peers. Living arrangements that worked when a child was four or five might no longer be practical when a child is seventeen and has a part-time job as well as a boyfriend or girlfriend.

> *"It is not the strongest of the species who survive, nor the most intelligent, but the one most responsive to change."*
> Charles Darwin

When your child expresses an interest in spending more time with the other parent, this is a question that should be explored. It is important for your child to feel that you understand her concerns, and it might also be important for you to consider some minor changes in the living arrangements. When a parent blocks this from happening, a child will often wait until she is old enough to leave on her own and will sometimes go, never to return.

In a study involving 820 college students who had grown up with divorced parents, most of the students said that their fathers wanted more time with them but that their mothers, who had custody, did not want this. According to U.S. Census figures, as many as one-third of children of divorce live in biological father-absent households. A report a decade ago from the American Psychological Association stated that "children from divorced families who either live with both parents at different times or spend certain amounts of time with each parent are better adjusted in most cases than children who live and interact with just one parent."

At a time when the research supports the need for both parents to be involved with their kids, and at a time when child specialists recommend the need for more fathers to be involved, what can you do to ensure that both you and your parenting partner are involved with your children?

A study by Edward Kruk, Ph.D., found that conflict is reduced in equal parenting households (equal parenting referring to parenting arrangements after divorce where parents seek to fairly and equally divide their post-divorce responsibilities towards their children) from the perspective of the children and parents, and a child's adjustment to divorce is furthered by primary relationships with both their mother and father.

4) Why did daddy (or mommy) leave us?

Similar to question #2, your child might also be looking for reassurance that you are not going to leave him. When one parent moves away, it is normal for a child to be concerned about the possibility of the other parent moving away as well.

> "We're taught to expect unconditional love from our parents, but I think it is more the gift our children give us. It's they who love us helplessly, no matter what or who we are."
> Kathryn Harrison, "*The Kiss*"

This can be a difficult question to answer because what you really might want to say is that your former spouse is a "jerk" or is "selfish", or a host of other words that I don't want mention in a family book.

The feeling of being abandoned by a parent is a huge blow to any child. Losing a parent through death can be devastating. In many ways, losing a parent through divorce can stir up the same emotions as the death of a friend or parent, and can continue beyond a normal grieving period because the absent parent is not dead.

Hopefully you will be able to reassure your children that their other parent will still be involved with them. It would really help here if you could provide some specific dates and times when their other parent will be spending time with them.

> *"They say that abandonment is a wound that never heals. I say only that an abandoned child never forgets."*
> —Mario Balotelli

Both parents need to reassure their kids that they will always love them and that they will always be a part of their lives. As suggested above, being able to provide some specific dates and times when you will be together can help to alleviate their concerns.

Sometimes the separation might be the result of a court order (such as a restraining order) that prevents one parent from having contact with the other parent and/or children. In such a situation, you have to be as honest as possible (without going into any specific details) related to what happened. Your comments need to be appropriate to the age of your children. If your kids have lived with an abusive parent, they will know what you are talking about without having to rehash the details of what has happened.

5. If I promise to be really good, will you get back together again?

Sometimes the underlying reason for this question is the belief, on the child's part, that she caused the divorce. It is common for children to believe that they did something wrong. As such, they also believe that if they can change their behavior (to become the perfect child), this might bring their parents back together again.

> *"It can be difficult to leave a long-term relationship, even when our inner-wisdom tells us it's time to let go. At this point, we can choose to let go and endure the pain of leaving behind the familiar to make way for a new chapter in our life. Or we can stay and suffer low-grade pain that slowly eats away at our heart and soul, like an emotional cancer. Until we wake up one day and realize, we are buried so deep in the dysfunction of the relationship that we scarcely remember who we were and what we needed to be."*
> Jaeda DeWalt

While most people understand that a divorce can cause problems at school, some children of divorce become more successful at school after a divorce. Part of the reason for this is an initial attempt by some students to please their parents (thinking this might result in them getting back together again), while another reason is that school can become a safe haven for children of divorce. At school, children don't have to listen to their parents fighting, or they don't have to experience an array of changes. School is predictable. What happens at school is consistent, and the routines that occur at school can help your children to feel comfortable and accepted.

> "Your children will become what you are; so be what you want them to be."
> David Bly

Kids benefit from rules and consistency. Unfortunately in some homes, rules change from day to day (and house to house) and the only area of consistency is the inconsistency of what is going to happen next.

While you should praise good behavior and a

positive attitude, your children need to be aware that they have not caused the divorce, and as such their improved behavior will not change what has happened.

U.S. statistics on divorce show that 13% of couples who divorce get back together again. This number would likely be significantly higher if it took into account the number of couples who separated (but never actually divorced) and then got back together again.

The Hollywood version of divorce sometimes portrays kids finding ways to get their parents back together again. Make no mistake about it: most kids dream of their parents reconciling.

In a 2011 article titled "Marital Reconciliation: Divorcing Couples With Children Open To Saving Marriage", a report that surveyed nearly 2,500 divorcing couples with children, found that either one or both parents in about 45% of the couples indicated that they still had an interest in a possible reconciliation. If at least one parent in almost half of divorcing couples has thoughts about getting back together, then there are a significant number of kids who will pick up on this.

A child's perfect behavior after a divorce or a child's nightmarish behavior might both be attempts to get her parents back together again. "If I'm really good, maybe my parents will get back together again." On the other hand, "If I'm really bad, maybe my parents will have to get back together again because I know that it takes two of them to handle me."

One of the real problems in responding to this question is that you don't want to support false hopes. This is particularly true of parents who have passive personalities who often tell other people what they want to hear, instead of what they really want to say. There is a danger for kids of such parents to be told "maybe" or "we'll see" in response to this question, not because the parent actually believes that he is going to reunite with his former spouse, but because he has the kind of personality that tends to please others even if this means avoiding the truth.

> "Sugar coating things makes people feel better, but it also gives them false hope, and it keeps them holding onto the wrong people."
> Sonya Parker

If you and your ex-spouse are serious about getting back together again, it make sense to spend some time in a neutral location (without your kids) to talk about the issues that drove you apart in the first place. It would most definitely make sense to talk to a marriage counselor to explore the issues that led to your divorce. Unfortunately some couples attempt to get back together again because they have "struck out" in their attempts to form relationships with others, or they ran out of money. These reasons rarely work because the adults haven't addressed the issues that led to the divorce.

> *"Grief is not a disorder, a disease or sign of weakness. It is an emotional, physical and spiritual necessity, the price you pay for love. The only cure for grief is to grieve."*
> Earl Grollman

In answering this question for your kids, you have to be both realistic and honest. It might be useful to ask yourself whether you might be fueling your child's hopes because you are secretly hoping to get back together again, or perhaps you are trying to protect your child from the pain of a divorce. Some couples move in and out of their relationship over and over for many years. This can be damaging to children because there is never any closure to what is happening. As stated earlier, if you are going to reunite, involve a counselor to help to resolve your issues, otherwise your home might become a battleground for continuing disagreements.

6. If you got divorced because you were unhappy, then why are you still sad?

Great question, isn't it? Perhaps when kids ask this question, they are doing you a favor. They are giving you a wake-up call. They are telling you that it is time to move on and let go of the past, although the question might also be a reflection of a stage of grieving that you are experiencing.

As we explored in the last chapter, there are various stages in grieving. Unfortunately, in divorce you might just think you are getting past the anger stage when something happens between you and your parenting partner to reignite your fury. In addition, when most people divorce they envision moving on without any contact with a former spouse. When kids are involved, this is rarely how things work.

Divorce generally results in a change of financial circumstances. Financial problems can contribute to being anxious and unhappy. As well, being a single parent might leave you exhausted. Yes, there are realistic excuses as to why you might still be unhappy, but perhaps you really need to take a closer look at how you are handling things. What are you doing to move towards a happier life?

When your kids ask you why you are still sad,

this could be the perfect opportunity to talk to them about some of the stages of grieving. You could explain that divorce is a form of loss and this can cause pain, anger and sadness. You could explain that it is necessary to feel the pain until it disappears. You could also explain that different people grieve in different ways and that grieving takes time. As you talk about your own grieving, this can be helpful to your kids in helping them to better understand what they are experiencing. You could also state that you are moving away from sadness to become happy, but this will take a little time.

> *"People spend too much time finding other people to blame, too much energy for not being what they are capable of being, and not enough energy putting themselves on the line, growing out of the past, and getting on with their lives."*
> J. Michael Straczynski

Your kids often see you in a way that is different than your own perception. If your children tell you that you are still sad or angry a year or two after the divorce, maybe it's time to get some help. Instead of giving your kids a boatload of excuses, maybe you need to tell them they are correct and what you need to do is better handle the loss you have experienced.

You could set a positive example for your children by joining a club or doing yoga or some other physical activity. If you don't have the time to leave the house to participate in any of these activities, there are exercise or meditation programs (available on TV or the internet) to help you in the comfort of your own home.

If you are sad (or depressed) to the point that this is interfering with your relationship with your kids or even impacting what is happening at work, this might be a signal that you need to make an appointment to see a therapist. Divorce can result in disabling pain; finding solutions to your own unhappiness can be very beneficial in helping your children.

7. Why do we have to move?

This question might also be rephrased as, "Why do we have less money?"

While some parents might want to say it's because your other parent is refusing to give me support payments (or the other side of the story: it's because your other parent is forcing me to make support payments), your answer should avoid placing place blame on the other parent.

A better answer might be to talk about how married people bring in two paychecks in order to pay for housing, food and other expenses. This could even be an opportunity, depending on the age of your children, to help them understand a little about budgeting. Next you can tell your children that following your divorce there is now only one paycheck at each house to pay for all the expenses for that house.

One paycheck does not go as far as two paychecks. Kids can understand this explanation. The end result of only having one paycheck is that it often becomes necessary to move to a house that is not as expensive to maintain as the matrimonial home. Hopefully as you lower your housing expenses, your children might enjoy a good standard of living (you might find it useful to read my book *Live Debt Free* in this regard).

"When you don't feel healthy, stop the excuses and do something. Just go outside, walk, breathe. Life's too short to fall into a rut. You are in charge of you - treat yourself well, and it'll show."
Jessica Stroup

It would also be useful in looking at this question to ask your children about their concerns related to moving. They might talk about missing their friends, having to change schools, etc. If you are able to move within the same school district, you might be able to satisfy your kids' concerns about leaving their friends or having to change schools.

Sometimes there are creative things that can be done in this regard (although you need to involve your lawyer to ensure that the wording and tax ramifications of such agreements are understood by both parents). For example, agreements are sometimes made where the children remain in the matrimonial home and it is the parents who alternate weeks in living in the home. In between, the other parent stays in a hotel or with friends. Such an arrangement would be difficult to maintain for a long period of time, but if this helped to gain some security for your children until they finished their school year, it might be worth it.

Another consideration in moving is the ease at which the children have access to both parents. There are some advantages to both parents living in the same school community. As the children grow older they might even be able to walk to either house to and from school. This arrangement has the huge advantage for your children of being able to maintain the same group of friends regardless of which house they are staying at.

Some of the more difficult arrangements for kids occur when one parent moves far away although programs such as Skype can help to maintain regular contact as can a defined time (or times) each year when the kids can actually visit and stay with the other parent.

Regular contact on a consistent basis and an attempt by both parents to respect and support each other can overcome some difficult transitions such as having to move.

8. Why do you always want to know what is happening at my father's house?

This question could also be rephrased, "Why do you always want to know what is happening at my mother's house?"

"At the end of the day, the most overwhelming key to a child's success is the positive involvement of parents."
Jane D. Hull

Martha, who was twelve, said, "I feel like a spy. The moment I get home from my father's house, my mother begins with the questions." Martha went on to say, "She asks me things like what did we eat? What time did we go to bed? What did we watch on TV? What's his girlfriend like?"

Martha explained that there was a time when she readily answered her mother's questions, but not anymore. She admitted that once upon a time she told her mother exactly what she wanted to hear - that dad's girlfriend was not very nice. But now she knows that that is not true; "Dad's girlfriend is actually very nice, and besides she doesn't always ask me questions that I don't want to answer."

During one of our support group sessions, the students were talking about their living arrangements. Martha said she planned on moving in with her father as soon as she could do it without having to go through all the crap of involving lawyers. When asked by another student why she wanted to this, her response was, "My dad is happy. My mother is too depressing to live with. It is painful to be with her."

It is normal for your children to talk about some of the things that happened when they were at your parenting partner's house, especially if they are younger. The manner in which you respond to their comments can quickly teach them whether you want to hear about the fun that they had or whether you want to hear about the "dirt". If your kids think that you want to hear about the shortcomings of their other parent, you are teaching them that there is something wrong with enjoying their time with their other parent. This is not healthy. Kids need to have your permission and encouragement to love their other parent and to enjoy their time with him or her.

Jenna was a nine year-old girl who gave her father a detailed account of all the miserable things that happened when she was with her mother. Jenna's father encouraged her to provide every last detail of her unhappiness with her mother. Unfortunately for Jenna (and her mother), Jenna's father documented every concern that he heard even though in the end most of them had no factual basis (Jenna eventually admitted she had lied quite frequently about what really happened because it made her father happy to hear bad things about her mother).

After keeping a precise record of Jenna's comments for more than a year, Jenna's father proceeded to take the mother back to court in an attempt to reduce the time that Jenna spent with her. A child specialist spoke with Jenna about the concerns that her father had identified. After admitting that she had made up almost all the stories, Jenna blamed herself for everything that was happening. In her eyes, she was the cause of her parents' ongoing anger. She felt responsible for being back in court. And worst of all, she knew she had hurt her mother.

A problem like this can add years of further unrest between two parents. In addition, the guilt that most kids feel about being the cause of their parent's divorce will continue. In this example concerning Jenna, besides straining her relationship with her mother, she no longer trusted her father. Our goal as a parent should be to help our kids become happy and successful, not mistrusting and plagued with guilt.

> "Abuse manipulates and twists a child's natural sense of trust and love. Her innocent feelings are belittled or mocked and she learns to ignore her feelings. The only recourse is to shut down. Feelings go underground."
> Laura Davis

The obvious exception to what has been presented so far in answering this question would be if you have suspicions of actual abuse occurring at the other house. If this occurs, you should contact the appropriate authorities. Child abuse is a serious crime and needs to be handled by professionals who can best help your child recover from the experience and prevent it from happening again. In many communities there are child and family services agencies where there are trained workers to handle abuse situations. If you are unsure what to do, you can contact a worker at one of these agencies by telephone to explain what you have heard (or seen). The worker can then give you her interpretation as to whether what is happening constitutes abuse and how to best proceed with your concerns.

9. Now that you're divorced, why can't you stop fighting?

In the previous chapter we explored the various stages of grieving. Anger was identified as being a normal reaction. Add to this the feeling of abandonment that some adults experience, and also add the jealousy that new relationships can cause. One mother said, "He doesn't deserve to have happy time with my children. He broke up our marriage and caused me and my children a great amount of pain."

The pain of divorce doesn't go away easily for adults, especially if one parent feels like the other person was to blame for the divorce. Unfortunately, arguing in front of the children causes anxiety for them and prevents them from handling the divorce in a positive manner.

Kent and Julie found themselves arguing every time they saw each other after their divorce. Their kids were constantly caught in the crossfire. After one of their children brought this to the attention of a family counselor, Kent and Julie realized the pain they were causing their kids. A decision was made to communicate any concerns to each other by email or text, and keep any conversations in person short and positive.

After a few weeks of trying this approach, it worked very well for them. Without the emotional triggers that often occurred when they presented their concerns to each other in person, email provided an opportunity to communicate effectively without experiencing the emotional triggers. Kent and Julie agreed that the past few weeks had been one of the more peaceful times in their divorce. There are a variety of ways for parents to communicate with each other. If person-to-person tends to get heated with one approach, consider a different way of communicating.

If your kids mention their concerns about your fighting, you could thank them for bringing this to your attention. In replying to their concerns, you could talk about some of the confusing emotions (guilt, pain) that you sometimes experience and how these can lead to outbursts with your parenting partner. It is likely that your child also experiences some of the same emotions. You could explain that you are going to find some positive ways to deal with these emotions such as exercise, yoga, hobbies, talking to a counselor, etc. As your child sees you attempting to deal with your pain in an appropriate manner, this can be very helpful to him in following your example. Best of all, once you are able to reduce and even eliminate public fights with your parenting partner, your child will have proof that there are appropriate ways to deal with emotional concerns.

Sometimes when parents are unable to communicate in an appropriate manner, kids become their messengers. This is not a healthy approach. This can create stress for your children, especially when the parent involved expresses his anger at the "messenger".

For example, you want to take your kids to a play, but the play is only on at a time when your children are with their other parent. I stress the word "only" because some parents constantly arrange special events with their children at times when the other parent is caring for them. In fairness to your kids and their other parent, you should avoid taking the children away from their time with their other parent as much as possible. But, if there is some special occasion that will "only" occur during this time, talk to your parenting partner about this.

"Forgiveness is not always easy. A times, it feels more painful than the wound we suffered, to forgive the one that inflicted it. And yet, there is no peace without forgiveness."
Marianne Williamson

Don't use your kids as messengers. This can place them in the middle of an awkward situation and cause pain for them. Some parents meet in a coffee shop once a month to talk about their kids and their schedule for the upcoming month. What a wonderful way to show their kids that they are united in caring for them.

> *"Any problem, big or small, within a family, always seems to start with bad communication. Someone isn't listening."*
> Emma Thompson

In an article titled "Communicating With Children" (on the website www.kidsbehaviour.co.uk), the author Beth Morrisey states: "Communicating with children requires certain skills. Parents must remember that children are still learning and developing so being able to communicate with them on their own level is imperative. In particular, parents must remember to use vocabulary that can be understood by their child, a calm tone and body language that will not send mixed messages. Parents should also allow plenty of time each day to speak with their children and stay involved in each other's lives."

In another article by Kristin Zolten and Nicholas Long from the Center of Effective Parenting, we read, "It is very important for parents to be able to communicate openly and effectively with their children. Open, effective communication benefits not only the children but every member of the family. Relationships between parents and their children are greatly improved when there is effective communication taking place. Children learn how to communicate by watching their parents. If parents communicate openly and effectively, chances are that their children will, too. Good communication skills will benefit children for their entire lives. When children feel that they are heard and understood by their parents, this is a boast to their self-esteem."

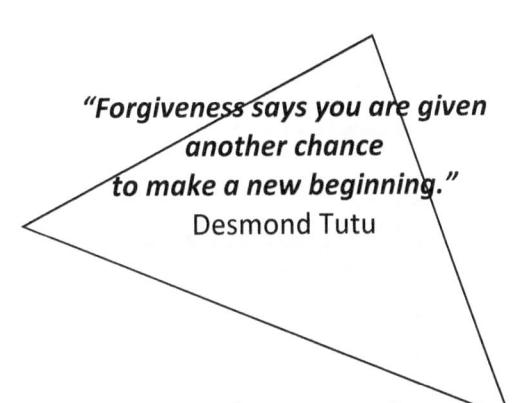

"Forgiveness says you are given another chance to make a new beginning."
Desmond Tutu

For many divorced parents, there might come a time when forgiveness will be the factor that helps your kids to heal. While it may not be easy to forgive an ex-former spouse who cheated (whether in an affair or in a financial matter), or for a multitude of other reasons, holding on to anger may begin to cause emotional and physical (and spiritual) problems for you. Being able to forgive can help to let go of the anger. Some studies have shown that parents who are unable to forgive an ex-spouse are more likely to take out their anger on their children through negative behaviors and harsh discipline.

In the previous chapter of this book we looked at the stages of grieving. Forgiveness might very well be a part of the acceptance stage. Forgiveness doesn't mean you have to agree with what the other person has done, or even forget about it. Forgiveness is more about acknowledging the pain that you have felt. It is the beginning of taking control of your life instead of letting some past event continue to control your thoughts and possibly even your actions.

10. What did I do wrong?

It is rare that any parents would actually blame their children for their divorce so this question is often a surprise to most parents.

Given the ego-centered nature of childhood (children believe that the world revolves around them), it is normal for them to think they are in some way responsible for whatever is happening in a family. When parents get a divorce, a child instinctively believes that somehow he/she has done something wrong to cause it. In their normal fantasy life children often believe that they can make things magically happen. Kids might indeed believe that they have the power to make their parents happy or make them sad. How many times do we reinforce this thinking when we say something along the lines of, "You make me so happy." If a child believes she can cause you to be happy, then she can certainly believe that she caused your divorce and your sadness.

Five year-old Billy said, "I didn't eat my vegetables at supper and then my parents got a divorce. I caused the divorce because I didn't eat my vegetables."

Thirteen year-old Kim said, "My parents were always fighting about me not doing my homework. When they got a divorce, I blamed myself for causing it. If only I had done my homework..."

As irrational as these statements might appear to us as adults, children can be plagued by guilt thinking they caused the divorce. Even when children can't quite decide what they did wrong, they can still feel they were somehow to blame. For many kids, it is simply easier to blame themselves than it is to blame their parents. Kids want to believe the best about their parents so instead they blame themselves for causing the divorce (even though they might yell and scream something quite different in your direction).

Another reason why some kids blame themselves is related to the inability of some parents to accept responsibility for their actions. As a parent begins to blame others, the children hearing the conversation might interpret what is being said as an attack on them, especially if their names somehow popped up in the conversation.

> *"People tend to dwell more on negative things than on good things. So the mind then becomes obsessed with negative things, with judgments, guilt and anxiety produced by thoughts about the future and so on."*
> Eckhart Tolle

In an article titled "Because Life Goes On...Helping Children and Youth Live With Separation and Divorce" on the Public Health Agency of Canada website (www.publichealth.gc.ca), the following was said: "It is important to keep in mind that however you as an adult understand or experience your situation, your children will see and experience it differently. No matter what their age, children have a limited ability to understand what is happening during a divorce, what they are feeling, and why. Younger children see things from their own perspective, that is, they see themselves as the cause of the events. This is why younger children often blame themselves or invent imaginary reasons for their parents' separation and divorce."

In answering this question it is important to respond firmly that, "You did nothing to cause the divorce. Our divorce was the result of problems that your parents were having; you didn't do anything wrong."

In responding to your kids (if they ask what they did wrong), it might be useful in the conversation to say to your child, "Tell me something you think you did that makes you think you caused the divorce." This might give your child an opportunity to give you a glimpse into his irrational thinking, and assist you in him. Often, kids are like a radar system in the house. Whenever you are talking to a friend about your divorce, or talking to your parenting partner, your kids instantly tune into the conversation. Unfortunately they don't always hear the facts properly (or understand the facts). Instead kids often hear their names being used. They then begin to associate their name with some of the content of the conversation and with the emotions. As a result, they often piece together little bits and pieces of the conversation, filtered by their guilt and other emotions, to conclude that they have done something wrong that caused the divorce and the continuing unhappiness of their parents.

To protect against this from happening you must be very careful what you talk about related to the divorce whenever your kids are anywhere near you. All too often, a divorced parent will vent his anger about a parenting partner with a friend. In some cases, the parent forgets the children might be listening, although tragically in some cases the parent is actually hoping that his or her children are hearing how horrible the other parent is. Your conversations with others, if you're not careful what you say, can prolong the pain that your children are experiencing.

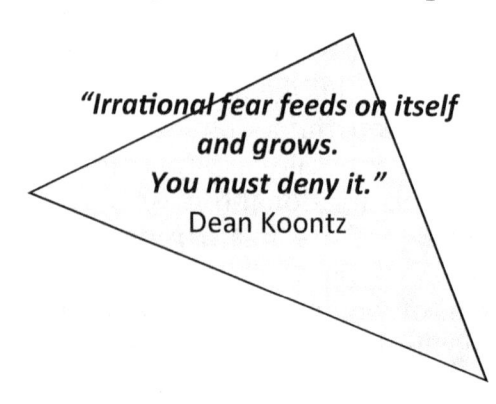

> *"Irrational fear feeds on itself and grows. You must deny it."*
> Dean Koontz

Another consideration here would be to inform your friends that they shouldn't "bash" your parenting partner when your kids are present. Sometimes a friend might just be trying to make you feel better by ranting about your ex-spouse, but in the process they might be creating further pain for your children.

It is easier for most children to believe that they are the cause of a divorce instead of their parents. When this occurs, and this perception can bury itself into a child's mind for a very long time, your child's self-esteem and happiness will be diminished. Whether your kids actually ask, "What did I do wrong?" or not, you and your parenting partner should ensure that your children understand they had nothing to do with the divorce. This is a question you might have to continue to answer, even when it's not asked.

11. Why do you say you are going to see me and then you don't show up?

Unfortunately some parents lack a sense of responsibility and are more focused on their own happiness than the happiness of their children (and in fairness to some parents, they might have careers that make it difficult to keep to a predetermined schedule). When this happens on an occasional basis, it makes sense to excuse the parent (heavy traffic, unexpected emergency at work, etc.) but when this happens over and over again, it is important to support your children and give them a chance to express their feelings (and it might be necessary to modify the visiting arrangements).

In an article in the *Federalist*, William V. Frabricius and Jeffrey Hall looked back on research studies and found that children want and do best with less regimented visitation schedules and more access to each parent. Findings were summarized by the following comment: "Children repeatedly insisted that being able to see the noncustodial parent whenever they wished and being able to see that parent often made their parents' divorces tolerable for them."

Comments from fathers in various studies talked about former wives who made it difficult for them to see their children during set visitation times. Fathers also talked about how mothers often turned their kids against them making it difficult to maintain a positive relationship with their children. One father said, "The tension and conflict, the anger that permeated all my contact with my wife and children was impossible to bear. She was really, really angry. Finally I gave up. It was hopeless. My daughter was caught in the middle. She was unhappy. She saw me as causing all this damage. After awhile I became afraid to make contact. My wife was perfectly content not to have me re-enter my daughter's life."

"Man must evolve for all human conflict a method which rejects revenge, aggression and retaliation. The foundation of such a method is love."
Martin Luther King Jr.

Many non-custodial parents talk about the pain and depression of only seeing their kids on an intermittent basis. In the end it is easier to stop seeing their kids. One father said, "I wonder if maybe it would be better to leave them alone and let them live their lives without me." There are a lot of fathers (and mothers) who really care about their kids, but walk away from them because there's too much hurt on both sides.

In a support group, one child said, "My mom left me when I was just a kid. I was five years old. I grew up with my father. I am still really angry at both my parents for allowing this to happen." Another person said, "My mother abandoned me when I was 5. Now I'm in my sixties. Throughout the years, I mourned the loss of my mother and felt inadequate and unloved as a child."

If there is one key theme that flows throughout this book, it is that the children of divorce need both parents.

Although some parents have realistic excuses for missing a visitation time with their children, a more frequent reason relates to the reality that a parent who only has contact with his children on a limited basis suffers a great amount of guilt and pain in becoming a part-time parent. Part-time parents worry that their limited involvement is hurting their children, more than it is helping them.

When a parent sees his children for only a small amount of time a destructive cycle can begin. The parent feels like he is a visitor rather than a parent. Even the kids often begin to wonder why dad (or mom) doesn't see them more often. Soon the parent, struggling with the pain of being rejected by his kids, finds it easier to disengage from them, sometimes moving far away and refusing to be involved (although in my conversations with such people, the pain often lingers. There is generally a sense of, "Did I do the right thing?").

There are some custodial parents who say things like, "My ex-spouse doesn't deserve to see my kids. He was the one who broke up our marriage." Unfortunately statements like this sound like revenge. They sound like the kids are being used to punish the other parent.

When we realize that the consistent involvement of both parents is an integral part of helping our children, we need to do whatever we can to encourage quality time for our children with each parent. In many ways, the very words "visitation time" that are often used with non-custodial parents reminds me of visiting someone in the hospital or jail. They don't carry a positive connotation.

When a non-custodial parent feels comfortable being with his children and when there is an effort by both parents to create seamless transitions, there is a better chance that non-custodial parents will show up on time to be with their children. As more and more parents have joint custodial or shared custodial arrangements with more flexible living arrangements with their children, this can be a huge positive shift in helping the children of divorce.

To return back to the original question, it is important to keep in mind that your comments and behavior when your parenting partner arrives to take the kids will speak volumes to both your children and their other parent. If you support your parenting partner, if you believe that the time that your kids have with this person is valuable, and if you engage in a positive conversation with your former spouse (and ensure that the kids are ready to leave), then you will be doing what is best for your children because you have established a framework that helps to prevent your child's other parent from feeling awkward about having time with his children, or your children feeling guilty about being happy with him.

12. Why can't we sometimes adjust the schedule of where I live so it better meets my needs?

This particular question is not so much about needing to spend more time with either parent as it is about the reality that as kids get older, their relationships with their friends (and their involvement at school, part-time jobs, and/or in the community) often take precedence over their time with their parents. For some kids, they will reach a time in their lives when it's simply easier to spend most of their time at one house or at least have the flexibility to make some changes when necessary to their living arrangements.

While these requests from our kids can make it

seem like they don't need us anymore, the reality is that even in continuously married families, many kids reach the point where they want to express their independence. They aren't trying to hurt a parent or withdraw their love; they are simply trying to take more responsibility for themselves (and spend more time with their peers).

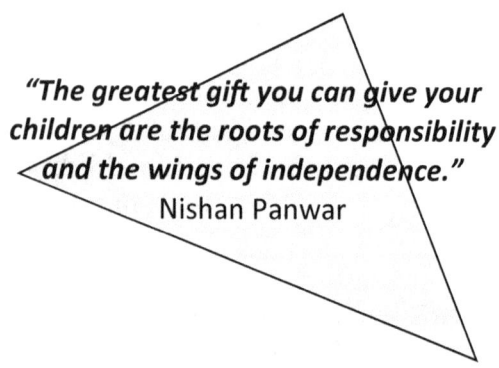

> "The greatest gift you can give your children are the roots of responsibility and the wings of independence."
> Nishan Panwar

In some ways when these requests occur, they can be seen as a good thing although they can make it more difficult to maintain a high level of contact, at least for one parent. Actual contact might have to be replaced sometimes by emails, texting, or other social media possibilities.

Some examples of what kids might be asking are things like, "I've been invited to go camping with some friends for the weekend. This will mean that I will miss being at your house. Is this okay?" Another example might be, "I have a new part-time job on weekends. My job is a lot closer to dad's house than mom's and because I start very early in the morning, it would be helpful to me to stay at dad's every weekend."

While these requests are generally small changes here and there, the reality is that some kids will eventually recognize that they feel more comfortable being with one parent more than the other (and this understanding can often have more to do with wanting to be closer to a boyfriend or girlfriend, than actually rejecting a parent). At some point, there might be a need to accept a teenager's decision to spend more time with one parent than the other.

As teenagers begin to spend more and more time with their friends, you might have to look for creative opportunities to spend quality time with your kids, even if it is no longer quantity time. Quality time could include dinner together, a sports event, a show, or a vacation together.

Even when your kids are establishing their own independence they will know if you care about them through your continued support and encouragement (and desire to listen to them). Every parent will face a time when their kids move out of the house. An unfortunate reality for divorced parents is that this might happen for one parent a little earlier than expected. Fortunately, as mentioned previously, there are various forms of social media to help you keep in touch on a daily/weekly basis, and a dinner together here or there can help you to maintain your bond with them.

For younger children there might also be times when some flexibility in their living arrangements might better meet their needs, but it is important not to let kids begin to jump back and forth from house to house, especially if the "jumping" is an attempt to avoid doing homework, a household chore, or facing up to the consequences of inappropriate behavior.

13. Will I be living with my brothers and sisters?

As a result of a divorce, children generally lose time with both parents. For them to also be separated from a sibling can compound their loss. This is a question that your kids are likely thinking about as soon as you and your spouse separate. If at all possible, your former spouse and you should reassure your children that they will be staying together. As suggested in other parts of this book, it is useful to reiterate that it is the adults who are getting the divorce, not the children.

When siblings stay together, there can be comfort for them knowing that they will be together regardless of which house they are at. Obviously the answer to this question becomes more complicated if one child has a very close bond with one parent while another child has a very close bond with the other parent. In such a situation, it is not unusual for the children to side with different parents which can fuel the conflict. If there is a reason for your siblings not wanting to stay together, this is a concern to explore with a counselor. It can be very damaging to the future happiness of your kids if siblings find themselves on opposite sides of a fight between you and your parenting partner.

14. Where is daddy (or mommy) going to live?

Most children are genuinely concerned for both parents. Although you might feel a great deal of anger and even hatred for a spouse who has left you, your children will often be worried about the safety of the parent who has left. Where possible it can be reassuring to your children to actually see where the other parent has moved. As you discuss future living arrangements, this could be an opportunity to outline where each parent is hoping to live.

Another part of this question is, "Will I have to change schools?" At a time when your children are facing troubling changes in their lives, it can be very helpful if they are able to remain at their current school (or at least stay there until the current school year is over).

More and more divorced parents are attempting to live in the same community which permits their children to easily access their school regardless of whichever house they are staying at. Where this is not possible, your children need to know about transportation arrangements that will permit them to attend their school.

15. Do I have to like daddy's or mommy's new friend?

Children generally have a sense of loyalty to both parents. A new boyfriend or girlfriend can interfere with this sense of loyalty. Children need to know that it is okay for them to love both parents. When this occurs, they are far more likely to be accepting of a new adult in the life of either parent. The manner in which a child responds to your new love interest is often a reflection of how you support her need to be able to love her other parent.

As suggested in the previous chapter, new relationships should slowly unfold for your children. Trying to rush your children into accepting a new person in your life can cause added stress for both you and your children. Having said this though, kids should be respectful of other adults even if they do not initially like them

16. Can I take my dog or cat to the other house?

Pets can be an important part of a child's life. Often a pet can provide a sense of comfort for your child when he is going through a difficult time. In a divorce, a pet can become one more form of loss if a child is unable to take his pet when he visits the other parent's home. It is often impractical to take a pet back and forth between two houses, but when it can be done, this might help to provide a continuing sense of comfort to your kids.

> *"Such short little lives our pets have to spend with us, and they spend most of it waiting for us to come home each day. It is amazing how much love and laughter they bring into our lives and even how much closer we become with each other because of them."*
> John Grogan, *"Marley and Me"*

Some parents rush out and buy their children a pet after a divorce. Before doing this, consider what is going to happen to the pet when your children visit their other house. If they can't take the pet with them, you should ask yourself whether it is a good thing to buy the pet in the first place.

Smaller pets like hamsters might help your kids to develop a sense of responsibility and caring, and be the kind of pet that could travel back and forth between two houses. If you have a dog or cat and the pet is able to move each time with your child, this could provide a strong sense of comfort and security for your child.

17. Will my friends be able to visit me?

As mentioned previously in this book, adults often keep the same friends after divorce (except where a former friend decides to support one parent over the other). Adults also tend to continue in the same workplace, once again maintaining a constant social network. For most kids, a divorce will result in moving, and often a change of schools. In addition to the other changes that divorce brings about in the life of a child, losing contact with friends is one more form of loss that can increase the intensity of grieving that a child is experiencing.

In deciding where you are going to live, if at possible attempt to find a dwelling that allows your children to continue at their same school, and allows your children to maintain the same group of friends. Where this is not possible, find ways (especially in the first month or two after you move) for your children to visit or be visited by their friends from the old neighborhood.

If you were to look in almost any book related to children and divorce, you would find information about the importance of both parents maintaining a relationship with their children after a divorce, but you might not find very much information related to children maintaining their friendships with their peers. One of the reasons for this is the assumption that kids are flexible and can easily form new friendships. Unfortunately that is not always true. As a school counselor, I have seen a significant number of kids move into a new school after a divorce, and struggle. These kids were already suffering the effects of their parents moving apart from each other as well as the effects of moving to another house. When kids lose their friends as well, this can be a significant blow to them.

During the course of a week, students spend a significant amount of time at school and in contact with their friends (if you really think about this, most kids spend more quality time with their peers than they do with you). For many kids, losing their friends is an issue. Finding ways to help your children maintain their contact with former friends can be very helpful in helping them to deal in a positive manner with your divorce. Children of all ages need to spend time with other kids. Familiar faces can be very helpful as your children begin to deal with other changes in their lives.

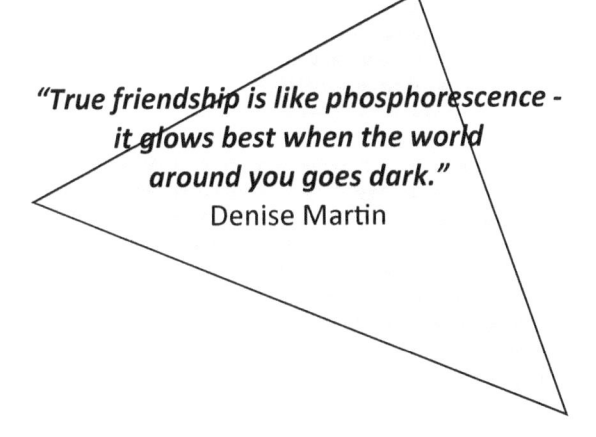

"True friendship is like phosphorescence - it glows best when the world around you goes dark."
Denise Martin

"Children are extremely sensitive to the emotions of their parents. It is important for parents to try to avoid overburdening their child with their own unhappiness or anger. It is also important to realize that at a time when children especially need support, warmth and firm, consistent control, many parents are least able to provide it. Parents should consider drawing on their own adult support systems and professional counseling when needed. It is important for them to get the help and support that they need to get through this difficult time. Children tend to take their lead from their parents. - if the parents are coping well, the child is more likely to do well."
Catherine Lee & Karen Bax; *Children's Reactions to Parental Separation and Divorce*

Some Final Thoughts

As stated in the introduction, the questions found in this book are those that have been most frequently presented to me by both parents and children related to divorce. The answers are based on my experience as a counselor in working with adults and children. They are also based on my own personal experience with divorce. Where possible I have included related research to support my thoughts.

Every child and every adult is different. We all handle the impact of divorce in our own unique way. I hope the questions and answers in this book can assist you in helping your children survive a divorce. I also hope that you will recognize that the individuality of some children and some families might impact the answers I have provided in a manner that I couldn't have anticipated. Where your child's uniqueness (and perhaps the out-of-the-ordinary circumstances of your divorce) don't seem to fit in with the tips and suggestions in this book, I recommend you seek professional counseling from someone who can meet with all of your family members to help you pursue a course of action that is best for everyone involved.

Divorce can cause disruption and pain. It can

can also provide an opportunity for growth. How you respond to a divorce is your choice, but the choice you make can most definitely impact the present and future happiness of your children.

> *"Each problem has hidden in it an opportunity so powerful that it literally dwarfs the problem. The greatest success stories were created by people who recognized a problem and turned it into an opportunity."*
> Joseph Sugarman

Also by Brian Harris

DISCIPLINE WITHOUT STRESS

Brian Harris, B.A., M.Ed.

Positive Parenting

Also by Brian Harris

TIME MANAGEMENT

Including 471 Tips To Help You Have More Time For Yourself

Brian Harris, B.A., M.Ed.

Also by Brian Harris

CHOOSING YOUR CAREER

Brian Harris, B.A., M.Ed.

A Self-Directed Guide to Help You Identify
Your Interests, Abilities and Values to Help You
Choose the Career That is Best for You

Also by Brian Harris

LIVE DEBT FREE

7 Proven Strategies To Help You Get Rich Without Having To Change Your Job

Brian Harris, B.A., M.Ed.

Also by Brian Harris

JOBS

A Practical Manual with a
Free Career Aptitude Test and . . .

Insider Secrets to Help You Find Your
Next Job and Improve Your Resume,
Cover Letter, and Job Interview Answers
to Help You Get Hired!

Brian Harris, B.A., M.Ed.

For Teenagers by Brian Harris

B.C. HARRIS
CYBERBULLY
SOCIETY OF SPIES

BOOK I

About the Author

Brian Harris is an award-winning teacher/counselor and best-selling author. He has extensive experience in working with children of all ages in elementary schools, high schools, colleges and universities. He has also achieved the designation of International Professional Speaker.

Brian lives in Burlington, Canada, with his wife and two teenage daughters. In addition to writing, Brian is a part-time lecturer in counseling at Queen's University. He is also an accomplished artist (www.bcharris.com).

Brian enjoys family trips and is an avid canoeist and scuba diver.

Additional information about Brian can be found at
www.cgscommunications.com

CPSIA information can be obtained
at www.ICGtesting.com
Printed in the USA
LVHW080130231220
674940LV00017B/985